CONTENTS

Introduction

KV-435-854

1. How the legal System Works — 17

Legal terms explained — 17

Using the legal system to resolve disputes — 19

The structure of the court system — 19

Civil cases — 19

Criminal cases — 20

The Magistrates court — 20

The Crown Court — 26

The County court — 28

Small claims in the county court — 32

The High Court — 33

The Family Division — 34

The Queens Bench Division — 34

The Chancery Division — 24

The Court of Appeal — 34

The Supreme Court of the United Kingdom — 35

Changes in Britain's relationship with the EU after 2020 35

2. The Availability of Legal Help — 39

Solicitors — 40

Choosing the right firm — 42

Using a solicitor — 42

Other sources of legal advice — 43

Financial help — 44

The Legal Aid Agency   44

Legal aid for civil cases (non-criminal)   45

The different types of civil legal aid   45

Who can provide legal aid services   46

How to apply for civil legal aid   46

Civil Legal Advice helpline   46

Legal services for deaf people   47

Legal aid for criminal cases   48

Free legal advice at the police station   48

Help before you're charged with a criminal offence   49

Help with representation at court   49

A Representation Order   49

Advocacy Assistance   51

Free advice/ representation at magistrates' courts   51

Paying court fees if you are getting legal aid   52

3. Solving disputes before legal action   53

Payments into court   54

Timing of court action   54

Damages   54

Damages for criminal injury   55

Procedures   55

Benefits and award limits   56

Compensable costs   56

Emergency awards   57

Funding   57

Appealing against a decision   57

4. Procedure in the Crown Court

4. Procedure in the Crown Court   61

The jury   61

Complaining about jury service   64

Inside a Crown Court   64

Court etiquette   64

The judge   65

Barristers   66

Solicitors   66

Clerks   67

The usher   67

The Crown Prosecution Service   67

The defendant   68

Witnesses   68

The press   69

The public   70

Court reporter   70

Dock Officer   70

Case study - guide to a criminal case   70

The procedure   72

Summary of the trial process in the Crown Court   79

5. Procedure in the County Courts   81

County courts   81

The Civil Procedure Rules   82

Circuit Judges   82

Registrars   82

County court jurisdiction   82

Small claims procedure   84

Tribunals   84

Civil cases in the county court   84

Case study outlining county court procedure   85

Summary of the trial process in the

County court   93

6. **Small claims-An Overview of procedure**   **95**

Types of small claim   96

Completing and issuing a claim form   97

Making a claim online   101

Response pack   102

Admitted or part admitted claim   102

Refuted claim   103

Judgement in default   104

Defence   104

Counterclaim   105

Directions issued by court   106

Enforcement proceedings   107

7.The Legal System in Scotland and Northern Ireland   **109**

Scotland   109

Hierarchy of Courts in Scotland   109

Small claims in Scotland-Simple Procedure   112

What is Simple Procedure?   113

How do I make a claim?   113

How do I respond to a claim?   114

What will happen to my case?   115

Further Information   116

Where can I get legal advice?   117

Ordinary Cause Claims-What is the procedure?   118

Which forms do I need to use?   118

How much does it cost?   118

Where can I get legal advice?   119

The justice system in Northern Ireland   119

Criminal and civil justice in Northern Ireland   119

Courts in Northern Ireland   120

Agencies involved in the justice system   121

Small claims process in Northern Ireland   122

Small claims   122

Enforcement of Judgments Office   124

Fees   124

Small claims online   124

Useful addresses

Glossary of terms

Index

Appendix-1-HMCTS Review of the Justice System

Appendix 2-Courts and Tribunals-Living with COVID 19

****

Introduction

Without doubt, the legal system is complex and daunting and many who go to court to either resolve disputes or to defend themselves when sued, will use a solicitor or barrister. Such professionals do not come cheaply. This fact, above all, can influence a person's decision whether to go to court. This book, by explaining the legal system and the operations of the various courts and personnel will hopefully give you an alternative and help you to defend, or bring, your own case to court. The book is very much an overview of the legal system and the processes involved.

However, if you require a more detailed step-by-step handbook directly dealing with becoming a litigant in person then you should read A Straightforward Guide to How to Be a Litigant in the New Legal world by Michael Langford.

Another consideration, particularly at the time of writing, is the fact that legal aid of all kinds has been heavily reduced, both directly to the claimant or defendant and to the legal profession with the result that more and more people are choosing to go down the route of do-it-yourself representation. Those who choose to defend themselves, or bring a case, are known as litigants-in-person. More and more courts are sympathetic to self-representation and judges will often help the litigant. Indeed, the Gov.uk websites offer advice to would-be litigants. This book attempts to throw light on the whole legal process by adopting a specific approach towards explaining what is involved.

Another major problem has been the pandemic that has caused an enormous backlog of cases that are waiting to be heard.

Problems arising because of COVID 19

The legal profession, particularly the court system has been badly affected because of the pandemic in 2020. At the time of writing, it the Coronavirus, has caused a massive backlog in hearing court cases and several suggestions have been put forward.

The setting up of Remote courts

The response to an investigation of the possibility of setting up remote High Court has been overwhelmingly positive, according to a report on the effects of the Covid-19 lockdown. Nearly 80 per cent respondents in the survey, which questioned judges, lawyers and ordinary people who have used the digital civil courts, thought that the system brought in rapidly to stem the spread of coronavirus had worked well. The response prompted one prominent legal technology guru to redouble his calls for a digital revolution, calling for "the widespread industrialisation of remote hearings". The report from The Civil Justice Council, which surveyed 1,000 people, found that those who had used the Chancery division of the High Court were the most enthusiastic – about 84 per cent described their experiences of remote hearings as positive or very positive.

One finding in the report that could provide ammunition to those lobbying against remote hearings is that they do not always save money. Some respondents reported that remote hearings were more expensive because of the increased time they were required to spend on preparation. More advance work was needed, they said, because preparing electronic bundles and documents was more time- consuming. Arranging the logistics of the remote hearings also ate up more time because equipment needed to be tested. Most negative responses were down to difficulties with technology and communication. Not being able to see the judge and other participants made it harder to engage and communicate well, making it harder to know how to present a case and when to speak. There were also complaints over difficulties in exchanging documents and taking instructions from clients and most respondents felt audio or video trials worked well for simple cases but not those involving complex or contentious matters.

Nightingale Courts

'Nightingale'-style courts are to be opened to help to tackle a backlog of more than half a million criminal cases that have built up because of the Coronavirus Pandemic. Ten sites have been identified after officials from the Ministry of Justice searched the country for suitable accommodations, including in the town halls and university lecture theatres where cases could be held within social distancing guidelines. Ministers are expected to announce the first tranche of venues where justice will be dispensed outside the usual court sitting, with more to be identified in the next few weeks. It is hoped that some of the new sites will be able to start hearing cases by August. Although the proposed venues have become known as so-called Nightingale courts, after the name used for the emergency coronavirus hospitals, Robert Buckland, the lord chancellor, would like them to be called Blackstone courts after William Blackstone, the 18th-century jurist. Blackstone was judge, jurist and Tory politician who made commentaries on the Laws of England which described the doctrines of English laws

Some think that Nightingale courts offer a short-term fix but that in the long term the solution to the problems of the justice system is proper funding after a decade of cuts. In their letter they say that they have identified empty buildings which could be opened for trials so that victims, witnesses, and defendants do not have to wait even longer than they did before the coronavirus crisis.

More than half a million criminal cases are now in a backlog which has built up after courts had to largely stop work because of emergency measures to tackle the pandemic. The number of cases waiting to be dealt with in magistrates courts in England and Wales has risen by 22 per cent while the backlog in serious cases handled in the crown courts has risen by 4 per cent. Outstanding cases in the magistrates' courts rose to 484,000 between March 8 and May 17, according to provisional figures released by the Ministry of Justice. The number in the crown courts rose to about 41,000. About 250 trials on average a week were removed from a listing before the case was to start between January and March 22, rising to about 400 between March 29 and May 31st 2022. Trials have started at several places Introduction 13 including the Old Bailey as restrictions have eased but the Ministry of Justice said the level remains low. Mr Buckland told MPs that he wanted to clear the backlog by Easter next year. He is also considering longer court opening hours, but plans are unlikely to proceed. The justice secretary was keen on suspending jury trials in cases such as "burglary and low-level violence that can be dealt with by a judge sitting with two magistrates.

Barristers strike

As we write, in May 2022, further problems have arisen with Barristers fighting back over the severe cuts in legal funding. In addition to the pandemic, thousands of criminal barristers in England and Wales are on strike over low pay and the state of legal aid funding in the UK (as at April 2022). The main issue is that of funding. From April, nearly 2,500 criminal barristers will impose a "no-returns" policy, which refusing cases passed to them by other barristers who were set to appear but cannot do so because another trial has overrun.

This is likely to have a ripple effect within the criminal justice system, stopping other trials and heaping "more delays on a system already suffering backlogs from the pandemic". The Daily Mail reported that more than 60,000 cases are waiting to be heard in England and Wales. Over the years, legal aid funding has been cut and frozen, with the CBA suggesting the real incomes for criminal defence advocates have fallen by 28% over the past two decades. According to The Times, 83% of criminal barristers "incurred personal debt or used savings during the coronavirus pandemic".

Data from the Criminal Bar Association (CBA) shows that 22% of junior criminal barristers have quit since 2016 and the number of junior barristers specialising in crime fell by 11% between 2016-17 and 2019-20, from 2,553 to 2,273.

A major factor for this is low pay. Newly trained criminal barristers earned a median pre-tax profit of just £12,200 in 2019-20, according to Garden Court North Chambers, a collection of human rights barristers. By comparison, the average median household income in the UK for the same year was £30,500.

Ministers 'dragging their feet'

The CBA has accused ministers of "dragging their feet" over implementing a recommended 15% rise to legal aid – a fundamental part of the justice system in England and Wales, which enables people who cannot afford legal representation to access a lawyer.

The rise was recommended as part of an independent review, which said an extra £135m a year was needed to nurse the sector back to health. It was described by the CBA as the "bare minimum needed to stop the system from collapsing", reported the BBC. But The Law Society Gazette reported last month that an analysis of the Ministry of Justice's proposals found that criminal barristers would only receive a 9% rise, rather than "the often quoted 15%".

So, it is important to be aware of the problems faced by both the legal system and the ability of people to take legal action. If you are in a position where you want to act, then it may be affected by both the problems arising because of the pandemic and the issues surrounding legal funding and the corresponding action by barristers.

**

Chapter one of Conducting Your Own Court Case deals with an outline of how the system works and who is who within the various courts. Now that GB has exited the European Union, the EU courts play a lesser role in the implementation of justice. The Supreme Court of the United Kingdom, which took effect from October 1st, 2009, is detailed. The role of solicitors and barristers is discussed in chapter two and the book points to other sources of legal help available. Chapter three outlines the importance of finding a solution to problems before they get to court, as this avoids an often long and costly battle. Chapters four to six outline the processes within the various courts and puts forward case studies which should help the litigant in person gain an idea of the processes involved. Chapter 7 is devoted to Scotland and Northern Ireland and how the court system and legal processes work there.

Overall, this brief but invaluable guide to conducting your own court case, presented through building blocks to the actual presentation of a case, should prove an indispensable aid to understanding the legal system before representing yourself in court.

****

Chapter 1.

How The Legal System Works

HM Courts and Tribunals Services is an arm of the Ministry of Justice. The agency is responsible for the administration of criminal, civil and family courts and tribunals in England and Wales. and non-devolved tribunals in Scotland and Northern Ireland. For more information on HM Courts and Tribunal Service, go to www.gov.uk/organisations/hm-courts-and-tribunals-service.

This book deals mainly with the legal systems in England and Wales and there are separate legal processes and systems in Scotland and Northern Ireland which are explained in depth in Chapter Seven.

Before deciding to embark upon legal action, whether you are doing so without the aid of a solicitor, or with a solicitor, it is essential to understand the workings of the British legal system. Only then can you begin to conduct a case or to understand how to get the most out of the system.

Legal terms explained

There is a detailed glossary of terms at the back of this book which deals with commonly used legal jargon. However, it is useful to highlight the most common terms right at the outset, as they will be used frequently throughout the book:

Claimant – when legal proceedings are brought, the person or persons, or organisation, bringing the case is called the claimant.

Defendant – The individual or organisation being sued, and therefore defending, is called the defendant.

Solicitor – a solicitor is the lawyer you will (or might) see for legal advice relating to your case. This person will have undertaken many years of study and passed all the necessary legal examinations. We will be discussing solicitors in more depth a little later.

Barrister – A Barrister is a lawyer who is a specialist in what is known as advocacy, i.e., speaking in court. A Barrister will have been called to the bar by one of the Inns of Court and passed the barristers professional examinations. A solicitor will instruct a barrister to represent you in court proceedings. However, barristers will not normally be the persons giving individuals legal advice in the first instance. The legal profession is, basically, split into two, barristers and solicitors, both of whom are lawyers.

Writ – A judicial writ is issued to bring legal proceedings. Civil cases are started in the courts by issuing and serving a writ. This document is completed either by an individual bringing the case or by a solicitor on behalf of the individual. It is issued by the court.

18

Litigant in person – a litigant is someone bringing legal proceedings or suing. A litigant-in-person is someone who chooses to represent themselves in court, without a lawyer.

Damages – Civil claims in the courts are for damages, which is money claimed from the defendant to compensate the claimant for loss arising from the action of default of the defendant. An example might be the sale of a good that has caused injury to a person, and it is alleged that the good was faulty at the time of purchase.

Using the legal system to resolve disputes

If you are contemplating any form of legal action, with or without solicitors, it is necessary to have a basic idea of how the system works. The more that you understand the processes underlying the legal system, the more effective you will be, both as a citizen and as a potential litigant.

The structure of the court system

The court system in the United Kingdom deals, in the main, with civil and criminal cases. They are heard in either the county court (civil cases) and the Magistrates and Crown Courts (criminal cases).

Civil cases are those that typically involve breaches of contract, personal injury claims, divorce cases, bankruptcy hearings, debt problems, some employment cases, landlord and tenant disputes and other consumer disputes, such as faulty goods. These are the cases that are most often dealt with by the individual acting as litigant in person.

Criminal cases are those such as offences against the person, theft, damage to property, murder, and fraud. These cases, if of a non-serious nature, are heard in the magistrate's courts. If of a serious nature, then they will be heard in the Crown Court and tried by jury. Although individuals do represent themselves in the Crown Court it is more usual to use a solicitor in these cases.

Criminal cases

The more serious criminal cases are tried based on a document called the **indictment.** The defendant is indicted on criminal charges specified in the indictment by the prosecutor. In most cases, the prosecution is on behalf of the Crown (State) and is handled by an official agency called the Crown Prosecution Service, which takes the case over from the police who have already investigated most of the evidence. The first stage will be to decide whether there is a case to answer. This process, called committal, will be dealt with by a magistrate based on evidence disclosed in papers provided by the prosecutor.

Magistrates' Court

Virtually all criminal court cases start in a magistrates' court, and more than 90 per cent will be completed there. The more serious offences are passed on to the Crown Court, either for sentencing after the defendant has been found guilty in a magistrates' court, or for full trial with a judge and jury.

Magistrates deal with three kinds of cases:

- Summary offences. These are less serious cases, such as motoring offences and minor assaults, where the defendant is not usually entitled to trial by jury. They are generally disposed of in magistrates' courts.

- Either-way offences. As the name implies, these can be dealt with either by magistrates or before a judge and jury at the Crown Court. Such offences include theft and handling stolen goods. A defendant can insist on their right to trial in the Crown Court. Magistrates can also decide that a case is so serious that it should be dealt with in the Crown Court – which can impose tougher sentences if the defendant is found guilty.

- Indictable-only offences, such as murder, manslaughter, rape, and robbery. These must be heard at a Crown Court.

If the case is indictable-only, the magistrates' court will generally decide whether to grant bail, consider other legal issues such as reporting restrictions, and then pass the case on to the Crown Court.

If the case is to be dealt within a magistrates' court, the defendant(s) are asked to enter a plea. If they plead guilty or are later found to be guilty, the magistrates can impose a sentence, generally of up to six months' imprisonment for a single offence (12 months in total, although this is being reviewed in the 2022 Police, Crime, Sentencing and Courts Act 2022), or a fine, generally of up to £5,000. If found not guilty ('acquitted'), defendants are judged innocent in the eyes of the law and will be free to go – provided there are no other cases against them outstanding. Cases are either heard by two or three magistrates or by one district judge.

Who are magistrates?

Justices of the Peace, as they are also known, are local people who volunteer their services. They do not require formal legal qualifications, but will have undertaken a training programme, including court and prison visits, to develop the necessary skills. They are given legal and procedural advice by qualified clerks. District judges are legally qualified, paid, full-time professionals and are usually based in the larger cities. They normally hear the more complex or sensitive cases. There are approximately 23,000 magistrates, 140 district judges and 170 deputy district judges operating in the roughly 330 magistrates' courts throughout England and Wales.

Justices' Clerks

Because magistrates do not need to have legal qualifications, they are advised in court on matters of law, practice, and procedure. This advice is provided by Justices' Clerks and Assistant Justices' Clerks.

Magistrates in the criminal court

Over 95 per cent of all criminal cases are dealt with in the magistrates' court. Magistrates hear less serious criminal cases including motoring offences, commit to higher courts serious cases such as rape and murder, consider bail applications, deal with fine enforcement and grant search warrant and right of entry applications. They may also consider cases where people have not paid their council tax, their vehicle excise licence or TV licences.

All magistrates sit in adult criminal courts as panels of three, mixed in gender, age, ethnicity etc whenever possible to bring a broad experience of life to the bench. All three have equal decision-making powers but only one, the chairman will speak in court and preside over the proceedings. The two magistrates sitting either side are referred to as wingers.

Most of the cases are brought to court by the Crown Prosecution Service (CPS) but there are other prosecution agencies such as RSPCA, Environment Agency, Department of Work and Pensions, English Nature etc.

Where a defendant pleads not guilty a trial will be held where the magistrates listen to, and sometimes see, evidence presented by both the prosecution and defence, decide on agreed facts and facts in dispute and consider whether the case has been proved beyond reasonable doubt.

Having found someone guilty or when someone has pleaded, the magistrates proceed to sentence using a structured decision-making process and sentencing guidelines that set out the expected penalty for typical offences. They will also take note of case law and any practice directions from the higher courts and are advised in court by a legally qualified adviser. For a single criminal offence committed by an adult, a magistrate's sentencing powers include the imposition of fines, Community Payback orders, probation orders or a period of not more than six months in custody (a total of 12 months for multiple offences). Magistrates may also sit in the Crown Court with a judge to hear appeals from magistrates' courts against conviction or sentence and proceedings on committal to the Crown Court for sentence.

Magistrates in the Youth Courts

Magistrates are specially trained to sit in youth courts, where procedures are slightly more informal than in adult criminal courts – for example, magistrates will deliberately talk directly to young defendants, rather than always through their legal representative. In criminal cases the youth court can deal with all offences committed by a juvenile (someone under 18 years old) except homicide, which must be dealt with in a higher court.

Sentences are quite different in that they specifically address the needs of young offenders. Young defendants should always be accompanied by a responsible adult when they appear in court unless they are mature enough to be considered independent of their parents.

Magistrates – Civil

Although most magistrates deal with criminal work, they also decide many civil matters, particularly in relation to family work. Magistrates' civil roles include dealing with cases such as non-payment of council tax.

Magistrates in Family Proceedings Courts

Magistrates undergo extensive training before they sit in Family Proceedings Courts where procedures are very different from the criminal courts; the court setting is much more informal and ideally takes place with parties seated around a large table. Cases – which can be both public and private – can be very emotional and upsetting for both parties. There is usually a fair amount of reading as both parties file statements and reports.

Magistrates always provide written reasons and can be assisted with extra information provided by a children's guardian, usually a specialised social worker.

District judges (Magistrates' courts)

District judges (magistrates' courts) are full-time members of the judiciary who hear cases in magistrates' courts. They usually deal with the longer and more complex matters coming before the magistrates' courts.

The Crown Court

The Crown Court – unlike the magistrates' courts, it is a single entity – sits in 77 court centres across England and Wales. It deals with serious criminal cases which include:

- Cases sent for trial by magistrates' courts because the offences are 'indictable only' (i.e., those which can only be heard by the Crown Court)
- 'Either way' offences (which can be heard in a magistrates' court, but can also be sent to the Crown Court if the defendant chooses a jury trial)
- Defendants convicted in magistrates' courts, but sent to the Crown Court for sentencing due to the seriousness of the offence
- Appeals against decisions of magistrates' courts.

There are three different types of Crown Court centre, based on the type of work they deal with. These are:

- First-tier centres – visited by High Court Judges for Crown Court criminal and High Court Civil work
- Second-tier centres – visited by High Court Judges for Crown Court criminal work only
- Third-tier centres – not normally visited by High Court Judges and handle Crown Court criminal work only.
- Circuit judges and recorders deal with Crown Court criminal work in all three types of centres.

Those defendants in criminal cases who are dissatisfied with verdicts may be able to appeal, as follows:

- from the Magistrates courts there is an appeal to the Crown Court on matters of fact or law.
- From the Crown Court, it might be possible to appeal to the Criminal Division of the Court of Appeal on matters of fact or law.
- Certain legal disputes arising in the Magistrates court or the Crown Court can be taken before the divisional court of the High Court.
- Matters of important legal dispute arising in the Crown Court can be taken to the Supreme Court (which replaced the House of Lords from October 2009).

Civil cases

Most people who buy this book will be taking civil action of one form or another. Increasingly, people are becoming litigants-in-person as this enables people to access the courts and obtain justice without incurring high costs. The only real costs are the court fees (which have increased substantially in 2014) and other incidental costs such as taking time off work and so on.

The County Court

The County Court deals with civil (non-criminal) matters. Unlike criminal cases – in which the state prosecutes an individual – civil court cases arise where an individual or a business believes their rights have been infringed. Types of civil case dealt with in the County Court include:

- Businesses trying to recover money they are owed.
- Individuals seeking compensation for injuries.
- Landowners seeking orders that will prevent trespass.

Civil matters, for example, pub licensing, can also be dealt with by magistrates. More complex cases or those involving large amounts of money will appear at the High Court; most civil cases take place in the County Courts. All County Court centres can deal with contract and tort (civil wrong) cases and recovery of land actions. Some hearing centres can also deal with bankruptcy and insolvency matters, as well as cases relating to wills and trusts (equity and contested probate actions) where the value of the trust, fund or estate does not exceed £30,000, matters under the Equality Act 2010, and actions which all parties agree to have heard in a county court (e.g. defamation cases). Most County Court centres are assigned at least one circuit judge and one district judge, but judicial numbers will vary. Circuit judges generally hear cases worth over £15,000 or involving greater importance or complexity. They also hear many of the cases worth over £5,000 but not over £15,000. As well as hearing cases, district judges generally keep an overview of a case to make sure it is running smoothly. They also deal with repossessions and assess damages in uncontested cases.

Although County Court judgments usually call for the repayment or return of money or property, anyone who does not comply with the judgment can be arrested and prosecuted. The court has a range of procedures to deal with enforcement of judgments.

Who sits in a County Court Circuit?
Circuit judges are appointed to one of seven regions of England and Wales and sit in the Crown Court and County Court within their region.

Fee-paid-judges-Various fee-paid (non-salaried judges) sit occasionally in the County Court – Deputy District Judges, Deputy Circuit Judges and Recorders.

District judges

District judges are full-time judges who deal with many cases in the County Courts. They are deployed on appointment to a particular circuit and may sit at any of the County Courts or District Registries of the High Court on that circuit.

A judge hearing a civil case

Before trying a civil case, the judge reads the relevant case papers and becomes familiar with their details.

Most civil cases tried in court do not have a jury (libel and slander trials are the main exceptions) and the judge hears them on his own, deciding them by finding facts, applying the relevant law to them – and there may be considerable argument about what that law is – and then giving a reasoned judgment.

Judges also play an active role in managing civil cases once they have started, helping to ensure they proceed as quickly and efficiently as possible.

This includes:

- encouraging the parties to co-operate with each other in the conduct of the case.
- helping the parties to settle the case.
- encouraging the parties to use an alternative dispute resolution procedure if appropriate and;
- controlling the progress of the case.

Occasionally, the parties will have agreed the relevant facts and it will not be necessary for the judge to hear any live evidence. The issues may concern the law to be applied or the terms of the judgment to be given. But often, written, and live evidence will be given by the parties and their witnesses, and the live witnesses may be cross-examined. The judge ensures that all parties involved are given the opportunity to have their case presented and considered as fully and as fairly as possible. During the case the judge will ask questions on any point he or she feels needs clarification. The judge also decides on all matters of procedure which may arise during a hearing.

Judgment

Once the judge has heard the evidence from all parties involved and any submissions (representations) they wish to put forward, he or she delivers his or her judgment. This may be immediately, or if the case is complicated, later. Civil judges do have the power to punish parties if, for example, they are in contempt of court but, generally, civil cases do not involve the imposition of any punishment.

If the judge decides that the claimant is entitled to damages, he or she will have to go on to decide the amount. Or the claimant may have asked for an injunction – for example, to forbid the defendant from making excessive noise by playing the drums in the flat upstairs in the early hours of the morning, or a declaration – an order specifying the precise boundary between two properties about which the parties had never been able to agree. The task of the judge to is to decide on what is the appropriate remedy, if any, and on the precise terms of it.

Costs

When the judgment in the case has been delivered, the judge must deal with the cost of the case. This may include the fees of any lawyers, court fees paid out by the parties, fees of expert witnesses, allowances that may be allowed to litigants who have acted in person (without lawyers), earnings lost and travelling, and other expenses incurred by the parties and their witnesses.

The general rule is that the unsuccessful party will have to pay the successful party's costs, but the judge has a wide discretion to depart from this rule. The judge's decision on this part of the case will be very important to the parties. He or she may decide, for example, that the unsuccessful party should pay only a proportion of the successful party's costs or that each party should bear their own costs. The judge may hear representations about this at the end of the case.

Small claims in the county court

A case in the county court, if it is defended, is dealt with in one of three ways. These ways are called 'tracks' The court will, when considering a case, decide which procedure to apply and allocate the case to one of the following tracks:

- The small claims track

- The fast track

- The multi-track

The small claims track is the most used and is the track for claims of £10,000 or less. Overall, the procedure in the small claims track is simpler than the other tracks and costs are not usually paid by the losing party.

Following a summary of the other courts in the United Kingdom, we will be looking in more detail, in chapter 4, at how to commence and process a small claim. In the main, (but not exclusively) readers of this book will be concerned with the small claims track and it is therefore necessary to outline that process in depth. We will also be looking, in chapter 2, at the legal help scheme. This scheme enables those with a low income to get free legal advice from a solicitor and assistance with preparing a case.

The High Court

The High Court will hear appeals in criminal cases and will also deal with certain civil cases. The High Court also has the legal power to review the actions or activities of individuals and organisations to make sure that they are both operating within the law and are acting justly. The High Court consists of three divisions, as follows:

The Family Division

The Family Division of the High Court will deal with more complex defended divorce cases, wardship, adoption, domestic violence, and other cases. It will also deal with appeals from the magistrates and county courts in matrimonial cases.

The Queens Bench Division

The Queens Bench Division of the High Court will deal with larger claims for compensation, and more complex cases for compensation. A limited number of appeals from county and magistrates' courts are also dealt with. The Queens Bench Division can also review the actions of individuals or organisations and hear libel and slander cases.

The Chancery Division

The Chancery Division deals with trusts, contested wills, winding up companies, bankruptcy, mortgages, charities, and contested revenue such as income tax.

The Court of Appeal

The Court of Appeal deals with civil and criminal appeals. Civil appeals from the high and county courts are heard, as well as from the Employment Appeals Tribunal and the Lands Tribunal. Criminal Appeals include appeals against convictions in the Crown Courts, and points of law referred by the Attorney General following acquittal in the Crown Court or where a sentence imposed is seen as too lenient.

The Supreme Court of the United Kingdom

A new addition to the legal structure of the United Kingdom, the Supreme Court of the United Kingdom was established by the Constitutional Reform Act of 2005. The court is the Supreme Court (court of last resort, highest appellate court) in all matters under English law, Welsh law (to the extent that the National Assembly for Wales makes laws for Wales that differ from those in England) and Northern Irish law. It will not have authority over criminal cases in Scotland, where the High Court of Justiciary will remain the supreme criminal court. However, it will hear appeals from the civil court of session, just as the House of Lords did before.

Changes to Britain's relationship with the European Courts after 2020

The Human Rights Act also requires UK courts, including the Supreme Court, to "take account" of decisions of the European What to Expect When You Go to Court 36 Court of Human Rights (which sits in Strasbourg). UK courts are not required, however, always to follow the decisions of that Court. Indeed, they can decline to do so, particularly if they consider that the Strasbourg Court has not sufficiently appreciated or accommodated aspects of our domestic constitutional position.

The European Convention on Human Rights and the European Court of Human Rights exist separately from the European Union. The Supreme Court's relationship with the Strasbourg Court is not, therefore, changed by the UK's exit from the European Union.

The relationship between the UK Supreme Court and the Court of Justice of the European Union (which sits in Luxembourg) has, however, changed. Two key changes are provided for in the European Union (Withdrawal) Act 2018 and related legislation.

First, the UK courts, including the Supreme Court, are not bound by decisions of the Court of Justice of the European Union made after 11pm on 31 December 2020. The UK courts, including the Supreme Court, may have regard to the Luxembourg Court's decisions if relevant, but they are not generally obliged to follow them. The Supreme Court (and some other UK appellate courts) are also free to depart from decisions of the Court of Justice of the European Union taken before 11pm on 31 December 2020. In deciding whether to depart from this retained EU case law, the courts will apply the same test that the Supreme Court applies when deciding whether to depart from its own case law. This means How the Legal System Works 37 that the Supreme Court (and other relevant UK appellate courts) will depart from a previous decision of the Luxembourg Court where it appears right to do so.

Secondly, from 11pm on 31 December 2020, all UK courts, including the Supreme Court, are no longer able or required to refer certain questions of European Union law to the Court of Justice (through what is known as the "preliminary reference procedure"). There are some limited exceptions to this. For example, the UK courts, including the Supreme Court, continue to be able to refer questions to the Court of Justice of the European Union about the interpretation of the citizens' rights provisions in Part 2 of the EU-UK Withdrawal Agreement.

****

Ch. 2

The Availability of Legal Help

For those contemplating taking legal action, there are several options. The first option is usually to visit a solicitor to gain legal help and to launch your case. However, it is a fact that many people are put off going to see a solicitor because of the costs involved. In many cases, unfortunately, this results in people being denied justice.

This book is designed to ensure that those who wish to pursue their own case without the help of a solicitor can do so. Nevertheless, it is very useful indeed to understand what it is exactly that solicitors and barristers do and what their role is within the legal system and to also understand what other forms of legal help are available.

The costs of launching a civil case in the county court are minimal, although this will depend on the value of the claim, and the process is relatively straightforward. Chapter 4 deals with this process in depth. However, many people would still rather work with the help and guidance of a solicitor. This chapter outlines the work of solicitors, the other forms of legal advice available and outlines the legal help scheme for those on low income.

Solicitors

Solicitors are trained to deal with a large range of legal problems. Large firms tend to be formed as partnerships and will have specialist solicitors working in defined areas, such as crime, family, landlord and tenant and so on. Solicitors are heavily regulated by The Law Society and must have no personal interest in the matter in dispute. Solicitors must take out compulsory indemnity insurance to indemnify them against negligence and the profession also runs a 'compensation' fund to compensate those who have suffered loss at the hands of unscrupulous solicitors.

Solicitors do not come cheap and will charge by the hour, charges being anything up to £150 per hour. There are often fixed fees for matters such as conveyancing.

For advice which they consider they may need a second opinion, solicitors will usually seek 'counsels' advice' which is given by a barrister. A Barrister is a specialist in advocacy, operating from chambers and costing anything up to £300 per hour. Often, high profile cases, such as tax evasion and libel and slander, will be conducted by barristers.

Anyone considering launching legal action will need to consider whether they wish to use a solicitor. For simple small claims, it is not necessary to use a solicitor as the process is designed to assist the layperson. However, the following instances may demand that you use a solicitor:

40

- Moving house
- Getting divorced (depending on the complexity of the divorce-many straightforward divorced are carried out in person)
- Getting arrested
- Other complex legal matters, such as negligence and nuisance compensation claims

Never use a solicitor without first obtaining an estimate of their likely charges in the matter. Some solicitors will attempt to be vague over such matters, but it is highly desirable for you to be assertive on the matters of cost estimates. Ensure that the estimate is in writing and is broken down and clear. Most solicitors now issue a 'client engagement' letter to their clients as recommended by the Law Society.

Solicitor's charges will principally be based on the amount of time spent on the case, as solicitors usually charge by the hour. The longer it takes, the more it will cost you. If the matter is complex, a solicitor will usually look at the case and decide how much they will do and how much a junior will cover, to minimise the costs. The notion 'the cheapest is best' is not always correct or advisable when dealing with solicitors, as the quality of advice and degree of organisation will vary according to the solicitors used. Usually, larger practices are better able to offer specialist advice and are also better organised and easier to get access to.

Choosing the right firm

The best way to choose a solicitor is by recommendation, for example one that a friend has used. It will be necessary to ensure that the firm that is recommended has the right experience to represent you adequately.

In some areas, all solicitors will generally have specialism, such as property conveyancing. However, for obtaining compensation for personal injury, or an employment law dispute then you will need to ensure that a firm of solicitors has this expertise.

The wisdom of using a solicitor

Solicitors are, generally, very thorough, and meticulous. They must be, given the professional standards and codes that they have to deal with and also because of the need to obtain all the facts. It is important that, in the first instance, you give the solicitor as much clear information as possible. Further ongoing contact by telephone is charged for. Most solicitors will monitor calls carefully and enter these in a log or journal. Time is money, so therefore you should ensure:

- All information is passed on at the beginning
- Do not contact the solicitor too often. Ask for regular progress reports to be sent to you
- Respond to requests for information from the solicitor straight away

- Require an initial estimate and notification when costs reach the level of the estimate

Aim for a friendly, professional, and open working relationship with a solicitor as you are both striving towards the same goal, that is to win your case. Finally, if you search online then you can access a wide range of solicitors and gain an indication of their specialist areas. A word of caution: you should always be wary of those solicitors who advertise on television. Many will say 'no win no fee'. Although this sounds attractive, the fees if you do win can be very high indeed. If you do intend to use such a firm, make sure that you understand the charges at the outset.

In some cases, you may be dissatisfied with a solicitor and will wish to complain or even sue. If this is the case then contact the Solicitors Regulation Authority www.sra.org.uk or the Legal Ombudsman (address at the back of this book) both of which can be contacted through the Law Society www.lawsociety.org.uk

Other sources of legal advice

There is no legal requirement to use a solicitor. People do so when they feel that they need advice in the first instance or feel that their case may be too complex. However, there are law centres operating in each local authority area, often offering free advice and specialising in family and community matters, such as health and housing www.lawcentres.org.uk. Citizens Advice Bureau also offer advice and can be found in each area. In addition, the CAB has online advice which can be accessed through their web site. This is very useful and has written advice on a wide range of areas www.citizensadvice.org.uk. Some bodies, such as the Consumer Protection Association, also offer advice, again either by phone or on line, about a range of issues affecting the consumer www.thecpa.co.uk. In addition, if you are a member of a trade union you may be able to get free legal advice from this source, some banks offer free legal advice, and it is worthwhile giving your local branch a ring.

Financial help

The landscape of legal aid funding has changed considerably in recent years. In 2022, the whole area of legal funding, as with all other areas of public expenditure is under intense scrutiny. The bottom line is that financial help for those needing legal aid has been reduced or in some cases eliminated. Many people will require financial assistance of one sort or another when either taking or defending a legal action. Lack of knowledge and difficulty in meeting costs are the two main reasons for needing assistance.

The Legal Aid Agency

The Legal Aid Agency provides both civil and criminal legal aid and advice in England and Wales:

www.gov.uk/government/organisations/legal-aid-agency

The Legal Aid Agency is an executive agency of the Ministry of Justice. It came into existence on 1 April 2013 following the abolition of the Legal Services Commission because of the Legal Aid, Sentencing and Punishment of Offenders (LASPO) Act 2012.

Legal aid for civil cases (non-criminal)

If you need help with paying for legal advice, you may be able to get legal aid. You will have to meet the financial conditions for getting legal aid. In some cases, legal aid is free. In other cases, you may have to pay towards the cost.

Civil legal aid helps you pay for legal advice, mediation, or representation in court with problems such as housing, debt and family.

The different types of civil legal aid

There are different types of legal aid which you can get which are:

- Legal Help – advice on your rights and options and help with negotiating

- Help at Court – someone speaks on your behalf at court, but does not formally represent you

- Family Mediation – helps you to come to an agreement in a family dispute after your relationship has broken down without going to court. It can help to resolve problems involving children, money, and the family home

- Family Help – help or representation in family disputes like drawing up a legal agreement
- Legal Representation – representation at court by a solicitor or barrister
- Controlled Legal Representation – representation at mental health tribunal proceedings or before the First-tier Tribunal in asylum or immigration cases.

Who can provide legal aid services?

Legal aid services can be provided only by organisations which have a contract with the Legal Aid Agency (LAA). These include solicitors in private practice, law centres and some Citizens Advice Bureaux.

How to apply for civil legal aid

If you're not sure whether you can get legal aid, you can use the 'Can you get legal aid?' tool on the GOV.UK website. Go to www.gov.uk. The Civil Legal Advice helpline on 0345 345 4345 can also advise you on whether you are eligible for legal aid. When you apply for legal aid, your legal aid provider should give you the leaflet 'Paying for your civil legal aid'. This can be found at www.justice.gov.uk.

Civil Legal Advice helpline

If you are eligible for civil legal aid, you may be able to get help from the Civil Legal Advice helpline. The Civil Legal Advice helpline gives free, independent, and confidential advice on the following matters:

- debt
- housing
- family
- welfare benefits
- discrimination
- education.

Legal services for deaf people

RAD Legal Services is a legal service providing specialist, independent legal advice in British Sign Language for deaf people. You must have access to a webcam and broadband service and you must be eligible for legal aid.

They provide legal advice and representation on the following subjects:

- debt
- housing
- family
- welfare benefits
- discrimination
- education.

You can get further information and help from their website at www.royaldeaf.org.uk.

Legal aid for criminal cases

Legal aid in criminal cases is organised by the Legal Aid Agency. There are different types of help you might be able to get, depending on your circumstances.

You should get advice from a solicitor who will assess whether you are eligible for legal aid.

Free legal advice at the police station

If you are at the police station, you have the right to free independent legal advice from a duty solicitor. This does not depend on your financial circumstances. Your request will be passed to the Defence Solicitor Call Centre. Alternatively, you can choose your own solicitor and won't have to pay for advice if they have a contract with the Legal Aid Agency. The Call Centre will contact your solicitor for you.

If you're under arrest, you have the right to consult a solicitor at any time unless it is a serious case when this right can be postponed. You must be given an information sheet explaining how to get legal help.

Help before you're charged with a criminal offence

You could get help with a criminal case even if you haven't been charged with a criminal offence. For example, a solicitor could give general advice, write letters, or get a barrister's opinion. This type of help is called Advice and Assistance.

You will get Advice and Assistance if you get Income Support, income-related Employment and Support Allowance, income-based Jobseeker's Allowance, the guarantee credit part of Pension Credit or Universal Credit. If you get Working Tax Credit, you might get Advice and Assistance depending on your income and personal circumstances.

If you are not getting one of these benefits or Working Tax Credit, you will only get Advice and Assistance if your income and savings are below a certain amount.

You should get advice from a solicitor who will assess whether you are eligible for advice and assistance.

Help with representation at court

There are three ways you could be helped if you need to be represented in court for a criminal offence.

A Representation Order

A Representation Order covers representation by a solicitor and, if necessary, by a barrister in criminal cases.

To qualify for a Representation Order in the magistrates' court, you must meet certain financial conditions. You'll automatically meet these conditions if you're under 18. Also, you'll automatically meet the conditions if you're getting Income Support, income-related Employment and Support Allowance, income-based Jobseeker's Allowance, the guarantee credit part of Pension Credit or Universal Credit. Otherwise, the financial conditions depend on your gross income and whether you have a partner and/or dependent children. If your gross annual income, which when adjusted to consider any partner or children, is over £22,325, you will not be eligible for a Representation Order. However, in some cases it may be possible to apply for a review on the grounds of hardship.

If you do meet the financial conditions, you'll usually get help with representation in a criminal case in the magistrates' court, if it's in the interests of justice that you are legally represented. This means, for example, if you are likely to go to prison or lose your job if you are convicted.

In the Crown Court, it will automatically be in the interests of justice that you are legally represented. But you might have to contribute towards the cost of your legal representation from your income or capital.

If you have a disposable income above £3398 per month (2022), you will have to make five contributions from your income. If you are late paying, you will have to make one extra payment. If you are found guilty and have capital over £30,000, you may be asked to pay a contribution from your capital.

However, you will not be entitled to legal aid representation if your disposable annual income is £37,500 or more and you will have to pay privately for your costs.

If you are found not guilty, your payments will be refunded to you. To apply for a Representation Order, ask for an application form at the court dealing with your case or speak to your solicitor.

Advocacy Assistance

Advocacy Assistance covers the costs of a solicitor preparing your case and initial representation in certain cases such as:

- prisoners facing disciplinary charges
- prisoners with a life sentence who are referred to the Parole Board
- warrants of further detention.

You don't have to meet any financial conditions to qualify for Advocacy Assistance, except if it's a prison hearing.

Free advice and representation at the magistrates' court

If you didn't get legal advice before your case comes up at the magistrates' court, you can get free legal advice and representation by the court duty solicitor. This does not apply to less serious cases such as minor driving offences, but it could cover cases of non-payment of council tax. You do not have to meet any financial conditions to get free advice and representation at the magistrates' court. The court staff will tell you how to find the duty solicitor.

51

Paying court fees if you are getting legal aid

If you wish to start court action, you will need to pay a court fee. You can find further information about court fees on the HM Courts and Tribunal Service website at www.justice.gov.uk. If you're on a low income, you can get help with paying all or some of the court fee. This is called a fee remission.

If you are receiving Legal Representation or Family Help (Higher) you cannot apply for a fee remission as your solicitor will pay your court or tribunal fee for you. If you receive advice under Family Help (Lower) where a consent order is being applied for, your solicitor will also pay your court or tribunal fees for you. You can apply for a fee remission if you are receiving:

- Legal Help
- Help at Court
- Family Help (Lower) except where a consent order is being applied for.

You can ask the court to tell you how to apply for a fee remission or you can get more information and the form EX 160A which can be used to apply for a fee remission from HM Courts and Tribunals Service. A very useful and comprehensive website that outlines all forms of legal help is that of the Citizens Advice Service: www.citizensadvice.org/law and courts/legal-system/finding free-or-affordable-legal-help.

Ch. 3

Solving Disputes Before Legal Action

If you are in dispute and feel that you need to revert to using the law before you do so you should try to solve the dispute amicably. You need to establish the facts of the matter and examine whether there actually is a dispute at all or whether the problem could be solved without recourse to the law. You also need to look at the dispute in terms of whether realistically you are going to win or whether you will be involved in a long and drawn-out expensive battle that you are unlikely to win.

You should ask yourself the following questions before committing a case to court:

- Is your case clear cut or does your opponent have a clear argument?
- What do others think about your case? You need to ask someone who is unbiased.
- What is the value of your claim/ Does it justify the time and expense of going to court?
- What are the likely solicitors (if any at any point) costs?

Payments into court

If you do go to court, it is worth noting that the defendant can pay a sum into court, representing the amount of money for which the defendant would settle. If the case proceeds and the plaintiff wins less than that sum, then the defendant will not have to pay the plaintiffs costs. You should always think carefully about accepting a payment into court and should take legal advice.

Timing of court action

Court actions can, by their very nature, be slow and painstaking. However, the timing depends very much on the nature of the dispute. In cases of emergency where an order is needed to prevent someone from doing something this can be made in a matter of hours. These are known as 'injunctions'. Most disputes, however, often take many months to go through the court procedure. So do not expect a quick victory, as the wheels of justice turn at their own pace.

Damages

The award of damages is the money which is won in compensation from the defendant. The judge in the dispute will make the order as to damages, which normally consists of a sum of money necessary to place the claimant in the same position as he or she was before the incident occurred. There is an obligation to 'mitigate' loss, which means that the claimant should take reasonable care to reduce the loss as much as possible.

Damages can be reduced where the claimant is at fault, for example where the claimant has added to the injury suffered by his or her own actions at the time and subsequently.

Damages for criminal injury

In cases where a criminal injury has occurred and compensation cannot be obtained from the perpetrator, you may be able to get compensation from the Criminal Injuries Compensation Authority:

www.gov.uk/guidance/criminal-injuries-compensation.

The CICA gives out compensation amounting to millions of pounds each year. The address of the Authority is found at the rear of this book. The eligibility requirements of the programme are that the matter must be reported to police as soon as possible after it has occurred. The matter must be filed to the CICA within two years. Those who can claim are:

- Victims of crime
- Dependants of homicide victims
- Foreign citizens

Procedures

A claimant can obtain an application from CICA, local victim support schemes, Crown Court witness service, local police stations or local citizens advice bureau. The application should be sent to CICA. The authority's initial decision should be made within 12 months, while reviews and hearings can take several months longer. Compensation can be paid as soon as CICA is notified that the claimant accepts the decision.

Benefits and award limits

The maximum award is £500,000.

Compensable costs

- Medical expenses
- Mental Health expenses
- Lost wages for disabled victims
- Lost support for dependants of homicide victims
- Funerals
- Travel
- Rehabilitation for disabled victims
- Pain and suffering
- Bereavement
- Loss of parental services

Emergency awards

Interim payments can be made where a final decision as to the appropriate award is uncertain. For example, where the victim's medical prognosis is unclear.

Funding

The programme is funded by the taxpayer

Appealing against a CICA decision

There is an appeals panel, which will hear appeals against the findings of the CICA. Details can be obtained from the headquarters of CICA.

What to do if you are sued.

In addition to deciding to sue someone, you may find yourself in receipt of a summons or writ through the post. The summons or writ will always provide for a written defence, which must be filed within a time periods clearly outlined on the document. If you do not file the defence then a judgement will be entered against you automatically. When receiving a writ or summons the following actions should be taken:

- Check to whom the document is addressed. It may be that it should be for someone else. If this is the case forward it on or return to the sender

- If it is for you read it very carefully indeed. With the summons will be a particulars of claim which will outline what the case is against you

- Note any time limits that you must adhere to

What form of action you should take will very much depend on the nature of the writ or summons. As we discussed, the case will either be civil or criminal. Most people are aware of the basic criminal offences, such as driving offences etc. A small claim against you could be for a variety of actions, such as breach of contract or negligence.

Most criminal offences require attendance at court. Minor criminal offences require attendance at the magistrate's court. Civil offences will require attendance at County Court if you decide to defend. If you admit a claim, then the matter can be settled by post.

In criminal offences, the judge will pass sentence. In civil cases, the judge will enter a judgement and decide on a level of compensation relevant to the action. If the defendant does not pay the money arising from the judgement, the following remedies are available:

- Send in the bailiffs to seize goods to the value of the claim.

- Attachment of earnings so that the award is taken directly from the persons salary

- Charging orders over the defendant's property

- Garnishee orders that can order money to be taken from a bank account.

****

Ch. 4

Procedure In the Crown Court

In Chapter 1, we discussed the nature of the Crown Court. As we saw, the Crown Court deals mainly with criminal cases. The process is heavily procedural, and each case follows a set pattern. It is not usual for a defendant or prosecution to present a case without the aid of lawyers. Some people, however, choose to do this and the following outlines a case and how it is conducted using a solicitor. The litigant in person will follow the same procedure.

It is highly advisable to have some idea of court procedures before a do-it-yourself presentation of a case. The procedure, however, will remain the same.

The Jury

A jury consists of 12 people and their job is perhaps one of the most important in the whole Crown Court procedure. A Jury is randomly chosen from the local public, between the ages of 18-70 and their job, in a criminal case, is to listen to all the evidence about the facts of a case. They will often have to make hard decisions concerning who to believe or not, when differing versions of what happened are given by the defence and prosecution. At the end of a trial, the jury retires in private and must decide the guilt or innocence of the person charged. The prosecution must prove the case against the defendant on each charge so that the jury are sure of guilt.

The job of a juror can be complicated and disturbing. Quite often, the charges are quite harrowing, and the evidence is not that clear. The juror, or jurors, must fight against their own prejudices and must avoid jumping to conclusions.

The following represents basic advice concerning the procedure relating to jurors.

The Court Service produces a booklet called 'You and Your Jury Service'. It also advises on the procedure for jurors relating to the pandemic. Further advice can be obtained from the Court Service website. This outlines the role of the juror in more detail.

If a court writes to a juror and informs them that they have been selected for jury service, they will send a letter that is filled in stating that either they are able to carry out jury service or asking for reasons why not. The court will:

- Let a juror know at least four weeks before they are needed

- Send a jury summons which sets out the rules about jury service and tells them if they can be let off serving as a juror

- Send a booklet 'You and Your Jury Service' which explains more about the duty of a juror and details of which expenses and allowances that can be claimed.

An information leaflet will be sent which includes a map, details of public transport and where to park, the times of opening, details of refreshments etc.

When a juror arrives at court they will be shown to a separate sitting room for jurors and shown a video which explains the job of a juror in more detail. They can also talk with a customer service officer in private if they wish.

How a juror's time is used

Some people may not be able to sit as jurors on certain trials because, for example, they relate to the defendant or the case. The court service always summons more jurors than they need because it is difficult to prepare for all circumstances. Normally, a length of service will be five days. Some jurors are needed for all five days others can be let off early.

The court service will:

- Try to use time as a juror efficiently
- Tell a juror every hour when you may be needed in court
- Let them go as soon as possible if they are not needed
- Let them go back to work on days or part days when they are not needed if an employer agrees with this.
- Give the juror a special number to phone (in larger Crown Courts) to find out if they need to come to court that day

Complaining about Jury Service

If a juror wants to complain about jury service, then a member of staff will first try to sort out the problems then and there. If they are still not happy, they can refer their complaint to the customer service manager. They can also write to the court manager. They may be able to claim compensation if they have run up costs because of court mistakes.

Inside a Crown Court

Court etiquette

All courts are formal. The whole ethos underpinning the dispensation of justice is underpinned by formality. This is because the events that happen within a courtroom are very serious, can lead to the deprivation of liberty and therefore must be treated with an appropriate gravity.

When attending court:

- Remove all headgear before entering the court. There are exceptions for religious observances.
- Enter and leave the courtroom at an appropriate time to cause as little disturbance as possible.
- Always keep quiet.
- Sit in the designated areas, which will be pointed out to you by the usher.

- Stand when the judge enters or leaves the court.
- Always ask the usher if you are in any doubt as to what to do.

The following activities are not permitted in court:

- Smoking
- Eating and drinking.
- Reading magazines and newspapers.
- Taking photographs.
- Making tape recordings.
- Using a mobile phone.
- Using a personal stereo.
- Taking notes (unless authorised to do so by the usher).
- Bringing an animal into court (except for a guide dog for the blind).

The Judge

The judge presides over the trial and tries to ensure clarity and fairness. The judge will decide on legal issues such as whether evidence is admissible (i.e., what the jury is allowed to consider). The judge must remain apart from other people in a trial and therefore has a separate entrance and a private office called 'Judges chambers. If you have decided to represent yourself without the aid of a barrister, then it is highly likely that the judge will provide some guidance without prejudicing his or her position.

Barristers

We have already discussed the role of barristers and solicitors in chapter one. Barristers (or counsel) are qualified lawyers who represent the prosecution or the defendant (in criminal cases) or the defendant or claimant (in civil cases). Barristers have special training in courtroom procedure and advocacy (presenting cases in court). They sit in the courtroom facing the judge and are responsible for explaining the case, arguing its merits and, most importantly, presenting the case by calling the evidence upon which the case is decided.

Solicitors

Solicitors are qualified lawyers. They work with their client and the barrister, preparing the case and collecting the evidence. Some solicitors have received special training and are qualified to act as advocates in the Crown Court. Solicitors can present cases in the magistrates and county courts. In a criminal case, the defence solicitor is appointed by the defendant. The lawyers representing the prosecution will usually be employed by the Crown Prosecution Service. Solicitors and their employees who assist counsel in the Crown Court sit behind them. In a civil case, each side chooses its own lawyers.

Clerks

The clerk, sometimes called the associate, looks after all the documents for the trial, and records all the judge's decisions and instructions, so that they can be acted upon. The clerk is responsible for some of the most important formalities: he or she reads out the 'indictments' (telling the defendant what he or she is charged with) ensures that the jury takes a solemn oath to give a true verdict according to the evidence and that the witness takes a solemn oath to tell the truth. At the end of the trial, they ask the jury what their verdict is. This is called 'taking the verdict'.

The Usher

The usher looks after the courtroom and the people in it including the judge and jury. The usher will also bring into court the defendants, witnesses and others required by the court.

The Crown Prosecution Service

The Crown Prosecution Service work closely with the police and:

- Prosecutes people in England and Wales who have been charged by the police with a criminal offence
- Advise the police on possible prosecutions
- Review prosecutions or possible prosecutions

- Review prosecutions started by the police to ensure the right defendants are prosecuted on the right charges before the appropriate court
- Prepare cases for court
- Prosecute cases at magistrate's courts and instruct counsel to prosecute cases in the Crown Court and higher courts.
- Work with others to improve the effectiveness and efficiency of the criminal justice system

The CPS, although working closely with the police is independent of them.

The Defendant
This is the person who has been accused of a crime and is standing trial for this in the court. In a criminal case sometimes two or more people are accused of committing a crime together.

Witnesses
During the trial the witnesses are brought one by one into the witness box to give evidence, i.e., to tell the court what they can about the facts of a case. First, the witnesses for the prosecution are called. Their evidence must be limited to things that they have seen or heard themselves. Experts may also be called on to give authoritative opinions on subjects such as fingerprints, guns, or medical matters.

Next, the witnesses for the defence are called. They may include the defendant and other witnesses, including, for example, 'alibi witnesses' (if the defendant denies being present at the scene and the witness can say where he was) and the defences own experts. If there is no dispute between the prosecution and the defence over the evidence of a witness, the witness is not called and instead the evidence is agreed and read to the jury as 'agreed evidence'.

Where a witness is vulnerable or worried about giving evidence, he or she may be supported through the experience by a member of the witness support team. They will look after the witness outside the court and remain in court when the witness is giving evidence.

More details about the witness Support Team can be obtained from the court office.

The press

The press or other representatives of the media usually sit at the front of the public seating area (or in other reserved seats) to report what happens in court for the benefit of the public in general. They are entitled to report any part of the court proceedings providing the reports are accurate and fair.

The court may order that they cannot report on proceedings if there is some good legal reason that they should not do so e.g., if children are involved, or matters of law are being discussed in the absence of the jury.

The Public

Any member of the public may sit in the public seating area to see and hear what is happening.

Court Reporter

Many cases are officially recorded as they proceed by a court reporter who is responsible for recording the evidence and the judge's summing-up (in criminal cases) and the judgement (in civil cases).

Dock Officer

In the Crown Court the defendant who is accused of a crime is accompanied by a dock officer who is responsible for his/her security. The above represent the personnel who are key players in the process of a trial. We will now look at a case study which will help put the whole trial process in context. is a case study outlining the procedures in a Crown Court trial.

CASE STUDY

Guide to a criminal case

The following constitutes the procedure in a criminal case.

Background to the case.

Peter, 18, has been arrested and charged with four offences-theft (robbing an off-licence of wine and beer) assault (hitting the shopkeeper in the face and breaking his jaw), possessing an offensive weapon (a knife) and damage to property (breaking a window and damaging shop furniture).

Peter told his lawyers that he didn't do any of the above and he has been set up by the shopkeeper, who knows and dislikes him.

He said that he had merely gone into the shop to buy wine and beer, had met a friend, and absentmindedly taken beer and wine whilst he was talking, and he was told by the shopkeeper that he would not be served. The shopkeeper attacked him, and Peter acted in-self defence. He also stated that he did not have a knife. There was a customer in the shop at the time who saw what happened.

Peter is represented by a solicitor who has 'briefed' or 'instructed' a barrister to act as Peters advocate-that is to present his case in court. Peter will have met the solicitor who is preparing his case on several occasions. He will probably meet his barrister for the first time before the trial.

The prosecution is also represented by a barrister briefed by the Crown prosecution Service.

Some weeks ago, Peter appeared before the magistrates. Then the prosecution solicitor explained the evidence against him. Peter did not have to say what his explanation was. The magistrates said there was enough evidence for Peter to stand trial in the Crown Court before judge and jury.

The judge runs the trial and must ensure it is always conducted fairly. The judge must decide what evidence can be allowed and

71

what cannot. He or she must advise the jury what the law is and, if Peter is found guilty, the judge will decide what sentence to give. He or she wears judicial robes (a wig and gown) and remains apart from everyone else involved.

As stated, the jury must listen to all the evidence about the facts. They will often have to decide which witness to believe or not to believe when different versions of what happened are given by different people. They must then decide, in private, whether the defendant is guilty or not. The prosecution must prove the case against the defendant on each charge so that the jury are sure of guilt.

The procedure

Prosecuting the case

Everyone who is accused of a crime must know and understand clearly what it is they are said to have done. This must be in writing. The clerk reads out each charge and asks Peter if he is guilty or not guilty.

The Defence

As the charges are read out, Peter says 'not guilty' to each charge. The jury is sworn in. Twelve members of the public, selected at random, are asked to swear that they will give a true verdict 'according to the evidence'. The juror has the choice to swear or affirm, depending on religious belief. If Peter has a good reason, he can object to any of the jurors. For example, if one is a friend, or a teacher at his old school he can object.

The prosecution opening speech

The barrister appearing for the prosecution will make a short opening speech to the judge and jury telling them what the case is all about. He must summarise both what the prosecution say happened and what Peter says happened.

Prosecution evidence

Each witness who saw what happened is called to give evidence. Usually, the victim goes first. So in this case, the prosecution calls:

- the shopkeeper
- the other customer in the shop
- the police who were called and who arrested Peter
- the doctor who examined the shopkeeper
- the forensic scientist who found Peters fingerprints on the knife.

Each witness swears to tell the truth or affirms that he or she will do so. The prosecution barrister asks questions of these witnesses first. The questions must not suggest the 'right' answer. These are called 'leading questions'. So, for example he cannot ask the shopkeeper 'did you see Peter steal the wine and beer' he must ask 'what did you see Peter do?'

Cross-examination

The barrister representing Peter can test the evidence of each of the prosecution's witnesses by asking any questions which are relevant to the case. It is the best opportunity to show that the witness is unreliable or cannot remember things clearly-or is even dishonest. When Peters barrister put it to the shopkeeper that he chased Peter and fell as he reached him, injuring himself, he admitted that he could not be sure whether Peter hit him before he fell, or it just felt like that, and he was confused.

If the defence disagrees with what a witness has said they must make this clear.

The prosecution

When the policeman who arrested Peter said he found the knife in Peters pocket, Peters barrister must suggest to him that, as Peter says that he never had a knife, the policeman must have placed it there.

The defence opening speech

Peter's barrister has finished his cross-examination and the defence is asked if they have any further questions. At this point he declines.

The defence barrister can make a speech but does not have to and is not allowed to if Peter is the only defence witness on his side. The defence rarely makes a speech at this stage – saving things for later.

The Defence evidence

The witnesses on Peter's side now give evidence. Usually the defendant, Peter in this case, goes first.

He does not have to give evidence but if he does not the jury can draw inferences from his failure to do so. The jury may think that he has something to hide, as he was the best-placed person to say what he believed happened.

Cross examination of defence witness

In this case, Peter gives evidence, repeating his story originally given to the police. Other witnesses on Peter's side also give evidence. His only real witness in this case was his friend Dave who he had met in the shop and talked to. Dave confirmed that Peter was notoriously absent minded and would not have deliberately stolen the beer and wine but was indeed only putting them into his bag.

This is the prosecution's opportunity to challenge Peter and any other witness on his side. This can be very direct and personal. The way in which Peter gives his evidence and replies to challenging questions can be the key for the jury to make up their minds on the truth of the case. In this case:

- Peter admitted under questioning that he had an alcohol habit and had treatment for this habit.

- Dave admitted that he knew Peter had bought a knife. He couldn't identify it though as the one the police said that they had found on Peter.

- The other customer maintained that although the shopkeeper was angry and chased after Peter, he had not seen Peter hit him.

Prosecution closing speech

The prosecution barrister makes a final speech to the jury explaining how he says the charges are proved.

Defence closing speech

The defence barrister makes a closing speech and explains to the jury why he says that the evidence does not amount to sure proof that Peter did what he is accused of.

Judges summing ip

The judge first tells the jury what the law is on each charge and what the prosecution must prove to make the jury sure of the case. He then reminds them of the important parts of the evidence from both sides. This must be fair and balanced.

Reaching a verdict

The jury will retire to a separate room. This will be guarded by a 'jury bailiff' who is an usher. The jury must elect a 'foreman' of the jury who will act as an unofficial chair and will announce the verdict in court. Juries must not discuss the case with anyone else, even if they go home overnight.

Juries are expected to reach a unanimous verdict. If they have tried for a long time the judge can agree to accept a majority verdict which must be at least 10-2. If that is not possible the jury is said to disagree, and the defendant must go through a retrial. If the same thing happens a second time the custom is that the prosecution is dropped, and the defendant is found not guilty.

The verdict

If the jury finds the defendant not guilty, then he can leave the court immediately as a free man. He cannot then be tried again for the same offence (although there are currently proposals to change this in certain circumstances).

If he is found guilty the judge must pass sentence. In this case, Peter is found guilty of theft and possessing an offensive weapon, but he is found not guilty of assault.

The judge now must sentence Peter. He will take everything he knows about the case into account. He will be told if Peter has any previous convictions. He will not sentence Peter until he has received pre-sentence reports from the probation service.

Plea in mitigation

Peter's barrister can explain to the judge why a light sentence is more appropriate than a severe one. He can produce references for him and explain any relevant personal circumstances about work or family life. The judge will also have a pre-sentence report prepared by a probation officer. All of this can be very important in helping a judge to decide between a sentence of custody and some other punishment.

Sentence

In this case Peter has past convictions for stealing and violence. He has been fined and placed on probation.

The judge has the following choices:
- Rehabilitation (probation)
- Community punishment (unpaid work on behalf of the community
- Custody in a young offender institution (Peter is under 21 so cannot be sent to prison)
- As Peter's offences include theft, violence and possessing an offensive weapon, and he has a previous conviction he is sentenced to eight months in a young offender institution.

The dock officer who has been escorting peter to the dock will take him down to the courts cells prior to transferring him to an institution.

Summary of trial process in the Crown Court

1. Prosecution – the charge is read to the defendant.

2. The defendant pleads guilty or not guilty.

3. The prosecution makes the opening speech.

4. The prosecution gives evidence. Witnesses are called.

5. The defendant's barrister cross-examines the prosecution witnesses.

6. The defence barrister makes an opening speech.

7. The defence calls witnesses.

8. The prosecution cross-examines witnesses for the defence.

9. The prosecution makes a closing speech to the jury.

10. The defence makes a closing speech to the jury.

11. The judge sums up the case.

12. The jury retire to reach a verdict.

13. The verdict is announced.

14. The defence barrister can make a plea in mitigation.

15. The judge will pass sentence.

****

Ch. 5

Procedure in The County Courts

In chapter one, we briefly discussed the nature of county courts. In this chapter, we will look at county courts in more depth and the procedure in a civil case, much as we looked at the procedure in a criminal case in the previous chapter. The case study outlined will help to outline the civil case procedure, specifically in relation to personal compensation. In the following chapter, we will look in depth at making a small claim for faulty goods and services.

County Courts

These courts were created by the County Courts Act 1846. They deal with most of the civil disputes, acting as local courts dealing with small claims. There are 216 County courts in the country. Generally, the courts deal with:

- Personal injury
- Breach of contract regarding goods or property
- Divorce and other family issues
- The repossession of houses
- Claims for debts

The civil procedure rules

County courts are governed by the Civil Procedure Rules which guide the actions of the county courts and of claimants and defendants.

Circuit judges

Circuit judges were created by the Courts Act 1971 and are appointed from barristers of at least 10 years standing

Registrars

Registrars conduct the administrative work of county courts. They are civil servants and must be solicitors of seven years standing. They have jurisdiction to try cases where the amount is less than £500 pounds

County Court jurisdiction

County courts have a range of responsibilities:

- Hearing cases and tort (negligence) up to £5000 pounds, although there is no limit if both parties agree
- Housing and landlord and tenant disputes-the court will consider cases where the title to land and recovery of possession of land, concerns a net annual value for rating of less than £2000 pounds. The court also decides on matters under the Rent Act 1977, the Landlord and Tenant Act 1954 (Business

tenancies), the Housing Act 1985, 1988 and 1996 and the Commonhold and Leasehold Reform Act 2004.

- The County Court will also hear matters where an aggrieved person has a statutory right or legal right of appeal in housing matters
- Considering matters of equity such as trusts, mortgages, and dissolution of partnerships where the amount is less than £30,000
- Hearing petitions for bankruptcy and winding up of companies with a paid-up share capital not exceeding £20,000
- Uncontested hearings under the Matrimonial Causes Act 1967, or Nullity of marriage. If they are contested, they will be transferred to the High Court
- Hearing disputes concerning the grant of probate or letters of administration, where the estate of the deceased person is less than £15,000

The jurisdiction of the County Court: cases will be commenced in the court in the area nearest to where the defendant resides or carries on business or where the cause of the action arises.

There are more than three times as many proceedings commenced in the County Court than in all the divisions of the High Court which deals with all other Civil Disputes

Small Claims procedure

The County court hears small claims actions up to £50,000 although if it is a significant amount, it is likely to be heard by a Tribunal. We will be discussing small claims in more depth later in this book.

Tribunals

The enormous growth in the work of the courts in modern times, coupled with the relatively high costs of bringing a court action, has led to an increase of the number of tribunals. Tribunals deal with disputes in particular areas of the law and attempt to do so in a less formal and speedier manner than would be possible through the ordinary courts

Tribunals are independent and impartial bodies, using the same rules of evidence under oath as the ordinary courts, although the Tribunal members may comprise both legally qualified and lay members. Procedures may be heard in a Tribunal having been referred from a court

Civil cases in the County Court

We have seen in the previous chapter that trials in the Crown, or High, Courts are usually trials by jury and the Crown Prosecution Service is involved. Cases in the county courts are cases held without jury, with the judge having the final say. This is because the county courts deal with non-criminal matters, small claims, between individuals and organisations. As with the High Court, the procedure is formal and regulated and there is a set process to go through when preparing and presenting a claim. In the county court, the person taking the case to court is called the 'claimant' and the person defending is called the 'defendant'. Neither party must be represented by a solicitor. Many people who use the county courts chose to present their own cases. As we have seen, although this can be the case in the High court it is not the norm.

In the next chapter there is an outline of the small claims' procedure relating to money judgements. In these cases, a solicitor is not usually used. However, in many other cases, a solicitor is used, and the following case outlines the procedure where a person is defended.

Case study outlining the county court procedure

Sandra was in the women's toilet at an airport. The airport is controlled by the British Airports Authority. She entered a cubicle and locked the door after her. However, when she tried to get out, she found that the door would not open. Sandra panicked, as she realised that her flight was leaving very soon. She decided to clamber over the top of the door, as her cries for help went unheeded. She stood on the door handle, which snapped, and she fell backwards, badly spraining her wrist and breaking her ankle.

Sandra decided to claim compensation from the BAA stating that they were negligent and to blame for the faulty lock. In short, they are responsible for her injury and subsequent missed flight and time off work.

On reflection, Sandra has decided to instruct a firm of solicitors to act for her. She knows that she can represent herself in the county court but has decided that the matter might get complicated and that the BAA will pay more attention to a firm of solicitors.

Before the case goes to court, Sandra's solicitors must fill in a claim form and send this to court. The claim form is the form used to start all cases in the county court and sets out Sandra's version of events and states why she is entitled to compensation.

The British Airports Authority disputes the claim and must present their defence. This sets out their case and states why Sandra should not receive any compensation.

Both sides may obtain evidence – that is statements from witnesses to support their side of the case, which sets out what they say happened.

As Sandra is claiming less than £15,000 compensation and the case should be dealt with quickly, it is heard in the local county court before a district judge. If it involved more than £15,000 or was seen to be more complicated it would be heard either in a county court by a more senior judge or in the High Court by a High Court Judge, but the proceedings would be similar.

As explained, there is no jury in most civil cases – so the judge hears the case on his or her own. The judge will have been involved in the early stages of the case making sure that both sides have their cases ready for trial. Judges now must 'manage' cases they are going to hear to make sure they are dealt with as quickly and efficiently as possible. In court the judge must decide based on the evidence what has happened and then must apply the law to settle who was responsible. If the case is proved the judge will decide how much compensation to award to Sandra.

In a civil trial a claimant does not have to make the judge sure that he or she is right. They must prove the case on a 'balance of probabilities. This means that their case is more often right than not. The judge will wear judicial robes and a wig and will sit apart from everyone else.

(See overleaf for case study)

**

The case

Claimants opening speech

At the outset of the case, Sandra's solicitor makes a short opening speech to the court which explains what the case is and what evidence will be called to prove it. The solicitor will also summarise what the defendant says the position is.

Claimants evidence

The claimant – Sandra – is usually called to give evidence first and says what happened. Other witnesses who help her to prove her claim give evidence. So here, her lawyer calls:

- her friend who had been waiting for her outside. She had eventually gone back into the toilet and heard Sandra in pain in the locked cubicle
- the doctor who examined her and reported on her injuries
- other people who had used the toilet in the recent past and had reported that the lock was sometimes jamming and defective.
- An important piece of evidence here, perhaps the most important piece, was the state of the lock-was it faulty or was it a one-off incident, not down to negligence.
- This is something an expert can decide, and the court has ordered a single expert to examine the state of the lock and

report on the problem. This saves arguments between different experts on what should be an uncomplicated technical matter. The expert said that, in this case, the lock was faulty.

Cross examination

This is where the lawyer representing the defendant (the counsel) will test what has been said by the claimant and witnesses. It is an opportunity to show that their memory is shaky, or the evidence was exaggerated or made up. The questions can be very direct or personal. In this case, Sandra accepts that she must have realised that the door handle was probably not going to withstand her weight and could break. Therefore, she knowingly put herself at risk.

Re-examination

This is a chance for Sandra's solicitor to ask further questions to clear up any confusion. However, he cannot ask about new things.

Defendants opening speech

The barrister representing the Airports Authority can make a short speech introducing the evidence he is going to call. However, often the witnesses are called straight away.

Defendants evidence

The witnesses on the Airport Authority's side now give evidence. In this case, an employee of the BAA gives evidence as to how often the toilets are checked for damage to doors. In addition, he gives evidence concerning any other reports of people being trapped. The employee explains that if Sandra had called out it would have been heard quite clearly by several people and explained that he had heard nothing until Sandra's friend had reported the problem.

The Airport Authority accepted the expert's evidence that at the time he inspected the lock it was faulty and the doctor's evidence about Sandra's injuries.

Cross examination

This is the opportunity for Sandra's solicitors to challenge the defendant's witnesses. The employee of BAA admitted that, as he was concentrating on other things at the time, he probably would not have heard the cries for help, unless it was very loud. In addition, the records did not show that the lock had been inspected or who had carried out the checks. So Sandra's solicitor suggested that there was real doubt about whether there had been an effective recent inspection.

Defendants closing speech

The Airport Authority's barrister now makes a speech to the court which reviews all the evidence and explains why the BAA says that it wasn't reasonable for them to be held responsible for Sandra's injuries.

He says that the BAA accepts that the lock was faulty, but they had carried out all reasonable checks and, at the end of the day, although Sandra was injured, in some respects this was down to her own actions not the BAA's negligence. The barrister will explain to the jury the relevant law and how it should be applied in this case.

Claimant's closing speech

Sandra's solicitor now makes the final speech. He explains that the BAA admitted that they were responsible for the lock and that the evidence shows that 'likely' they had not checked it properly to see that it was safe. Unlike a criminal case in the Crown Court, Sandra does not have to prove this so that the judge is sure-it is enough to prove that, on a balance of probabilities the locks were not checked. He also argues that Sandra should not be blamed for trying to escape when the problem was caused by the negligence of the BAA in the first place. He describes to the judge what the law is and refers to any relevant cases which have been decided in similar situations, whether they support his case or not. The relevant similar findings are called 'precedents'.

The Judgement

The judge now gives his judgement. Usually this happens straightaway but in more complicated cases the judgement can be reserved and given later when the judge has had a chance to consider everything in detail.

In this case, the judge said that this was a simple case. He decided that the BAA were responsible for providing safe changing rooms in the sports centre. He had considered the evidence about checking the locks and that in his view it was more probable than not that this lock hadn't been checked recently. Finally, the judge said that it was reasonable for someone trapped in a cubicle to try to escape provided their efforts were sensible. The decision was that the BAA should compensate Sandra. However, he also decided that Sandra had been at fault. She had contributed to her own injuries by her own negligence in risking standing on a 'moveable' object-the door handle.

The judge ruled that Sandra's own compensation of £4750 should be reduced by 20% because she had also been at fault. She was therefore awarded £3800.

The above is an outline of a typical county court case. It can be seen, however, that the procedures in the High Courts and country courts have one thing in common. They are bound by formality and involve a set procedure where each party can present their case, either through representatives or on their own behalf, and each can expect to get a full hearing. In the Crown Courts, a jury will, in most cases, decide as to innocence and guilt. In the county courts, the judge will do so. However, the processes are similar in many respects.

Summary of trial process in the county court

The claimant or the claimant's solicitor makes an opening speech.

- The claimant is called to give evidence.

- The defendant or the defendant's solicitor cross-examines the claimant.

- There is a re-examination.

- The defendant or defendant's solicitor makes an opening speech.

- The defendant gives evidence.

- There is a cross examination of the defendant.

- The defendant or defendant's solicitor makes a closing speech.

- The claimant or claimant's solicitor makes a closing speech.

- The judge gives his judgement.

****

Ch. 6

Small Claims-An Overview of Procedure

Part 7 of the County Court Rules governs the issue of the claim form. If a defence is not filed, judgement is entered for the claimant because the defendant is in default of the obligation to file a defence. If a defence is filed, the claim is in appropriate circumstances allocated to the small claims track and proceeds under the provisions of Part 27.

The procedure for small claims is informal. The district judge hears the case in a private room although the hearing is now open to the public if they wish to attend, (in practice this is seldom the case). You can claim fixed costs, your own personal costs, witness expenses up to £50 per day, and in certain cases expert fees for reports up to £200 (only if the judge gives permission to use an expert witness). Solicitors' fees are not awarded to the successful party. However, up to £260 may be claimed for legal advice if the claim includes an injunction. You should check these figures at the time of going to court as they are subject to change. This is to encourage members of the public to conduct their own case. The small claims procedure is designed for lawyer-free self-representation.

In certain cases, expenses for travel and overnight accommodation may be claimed. The Court provides standard forms for completion by the opponents throughout a case with the intention that for simple matters, you could present your own case. The same forms are available from the Lord Chancellor's homepage.

Types of Small Claim

Your claim may be for a fixed amount or for an amount to be assessed. In the latter case, liability for the claim is treated separately from assessment of the amount of the claim. In such a case, you would write on the claim form e.g., "not more than £3,000" when the claim is for between £1,000 and £3,000. If a defence is not filed or if such a claim is admitted, you would obtain judgement with damages to be assessed by the district judge at a "disposal hearing".

If a defence is not filed or if such a claim is admitted, you would obtain judgement with damages to be assessed by the district judge at a 'disposal hearing'. In most cases, you will know the amount of your claim.

Special Features of Part 7 Procedures

- The claimant is entitled to Judgement in default of the defendant filing the Acknowledgement of service and/or the defence, or

- Judgement on liability with damages to be assessed at a disposal hearing

Special features of the Small Claims Track

- Complicated rules do not apply
- The hearing is informal and not in open court although the public can attend.

Completing and Issuing a Claim Form

From 19 March 2012, there was an important change to administration of money claims. If you want to make a county court money claim you must send the claim form to the "County Court Money Claims Centre" (CCMCC) or if you don't want to use the CCMC, then you will have to use Money Claims On-Line (see below). This change was part of improvements to the administration of civil business. Cases will be issued at the CCMCC and where they become defended and ready to be allocated to a track, they will be transferred to an appropriate county court. Claim Forms can be posted to the CCMC at:

Salford Business Centre
PO Box 527
Salford
M5 0BY

Any enquiries on cases proceeding at the CCMCC should be made to the following:

For email enquiries: ccmcccustomerenquiries@hmcts.gov.uk
For e-filing enquiries: ccmcc-filing@hmcts.gov.uk
For telephone enquiries: 0300 1231372

It is important to complete the claim form as accurately as you can. Once the claim form has been served on the defendant, permission is needed from the defendant to amend it and if that is not forthcoming then you would have to apply to the court. So, ensure you have entered the details correctly and that you have named the defendant correctly. If the defendant is a business, then it is important to have the correct legal entity of the organisation. Is the business an incorporated company? If it is, then there should be the word "LTD" or "Limited" after its name. A limited company should have the registered company number on its headed paper and so you can use this number to check the full company name and registered office by visiting Companies House website. It is advisable to state the registered office of a company as the address where the court should send the claim. This should remove any doubts of service. You can of course always send a copy of the claim to the trading address after the court has sent it to the registered office. On the claim form there must be a statement of value. The statement of value should be inserted below the word "Value" on the front page of the claim form. The form of wording should be: "Value: £X plus accrued interest and fixed costs.

In deciding which level of court fee the claim comes within, the court considers the interest claimed to the date of the claim.

In a personal injury claim, for example, where you would be claiming general damages for pain and suffering, statement of value would be worded, for example, as "the claimant expects to recover between £5,000 and £15,000".

The particulars of claim must be verified by a statement of truth. The person signing a statement of truth can be guilty of contempt of court if they know that the facts contained within the document are untrue. A solicitor can sign the statement of truth in his own name but states that: "The Claimant believes......". A solicitor should check the contents of the particulars of claim with his client before he signs it on their behalf. If the statement of truth is being signed by an officer of a company, that person must be at a senior level, such as a manager or director.

On the front page of the claim form, there are boxes where you enter the amount of the claim. There is a box for fixed solicitors' costs as allowed by the court rules. These fixed costs can only be claimed if you have a solicitor acting for you.

There is a court fee to issue a court claim. The level of fee depends on the amount claimed. Below is a summary of fees as of April 2022.

If you know the claim amount

The court fee is based on the amount you are claiming, plus any interest.

Claim amount	Fees
Up to £300	£35
£300.01 to £500	£50
£500.01 to £1,000	£70
£1,000.01 to £1,500	£80
£1,500.01 to £3,000	£115
£3000.01 to £5,000	£205
£5000.01 to £10,000	£455
£10,000.01 to £200,000	5% of the claim
More than £200,000	£10,000

If you do not know the claim amount

Use the paper claim form if you do not know the exact amount-you cannot make a claim online. You will need to estimate the amount that you are claiming and pay the fee for that amount.

The policy of the Ministry of Justice is to make county courts self-financing which has caused a steady increase in court fees. If you are an individual and are either on a qualifying state benefit or your disposable income is below a certain level, you may be able to obtain a full or part fee remission, which means that you will not have to pay all or part of the required court fee. To claim for a "fee remission", you will have to complete the relevant application form and supply up to date documentary evidence regarding your finances. Fee remissions are not available for business. If a claim is issued through the Claim Production Centre, then the court fee is discounted. The Claim Production Centre is designed for those issuing many debt actions.

Freezing Orders

A creditor can prevent a debtor from moving assets out of reach by applying for a freezing order. A freezing order is an injunction which prevents a party from removing assets out of the country or from dealing with the assets. Application for a freezing injunction are usually made to the High Court, but there are exceptions where an order can be granted by a county court such as where it is sought to aid execution after judgment. If you are considering applying for a freezing order, it is strongly recommended that you seek the assistance of a solicitor.

Making a Claim Online

Those with access to the internet can start a claim for money online. To start the claim, you need to visit the Court Service website: www.moneyclaim.gov.uk/web/mcol/welcome

The County Court Money Claims Centre is open to individuals, solicitors, and companies. It has the advantage that it operates 24 hours a day, 7 days a week and so you can go online anytime and monitor the progress of your case. Also, a change to the court rules that came into force in April 2009 enables more detailed particulars of claim to be served separately within 14 days of issuing the claim. This removed the disadvantage of the online claim form having limited space for giving particulars of the claim.

To use "Money Claims Online", the claim must be for a fixed amount that is less than £100,000. You must pay for the court fees by credit or debit card. Users of this system cannot obtain an exemption from court fees.

Response Pack

The court will then serve (i.e., post) the claim form on the defendant with a "RESPONSE Pack" containing four forms, a Form of Acknowledgement, a Form of Admission (N9A), a form for filing a Defence (N9B) and a form for filing a Counterclaim (N9B)

Admitted or Part Admitted Claims: Part 14

The DEFENDANT may either

- Admit/Part admit the claim with an offer to pay immediately. The court will enter judgement.
- Admit/Part admit the claim with an offer to pay in instalments.
- If the claim is part admitted, a defence should be filed to show why part of the claim is not admitted

- If the claim is for an unspecified amount i.e., an amount to be assessed, the defendant can admit the claim and make an offer.

The CLAIMANT may then
- File an application for judgement of the admitted claim
- Accept or reject an offer of instalments on an admitted claim. If you reject the instalments offered, the court clerk will assess the defendant's statement of means and make an order for instalments. If you are dissatisfied with the clerk's decision, you may apply to the district judge for a determination.
- Reject a part admission; in which case the claim proceeds as if defended. And the defendant should file a defence.
- In the case of an admitted claim with the "amount to be assessed", you should apply for judgement to be entered for liability. The court will schedule a "disposal hearing" to determine the amount of the claim or damages payable. If an offer is made in respect of a claim for an unspecified sum, the offer may be either accepted or rejected. If it is rejected, the court will proceed to a "disposal hearing" for damages to be assessed

Refuted Claims
The defendant may as an alternative to admitting the claim:

- File the acknowledgement requesting 28 days to file the defence: or
- File a defence within 14 days; and/or
- File a counterclaim against the claimant; and/or
- Issue a Part 20 Notice against a non-party or a contribution notice against a co-defendant

Judgement in Default

If the defendant does not file a defence within 14 days of the date of service of the claim (or 28 days from filing the acknowledgement of service), the court will at the request of the claimant order judgement in the claimant's favour without a hearing. This is judgement "in default" of the defendant filing a defence. The claimant should file a request for a default judgement after the period has lapsed. If the amount of the claim is not specified on the claim form, then as indicated above, you should file the request and the court will order judgement for the claimant with damages to be assessed at a disposal hearing.

Defence

The defence is a statement of case and Part 16 requires that it states (a) which allegations in the particulars of claim are denied (b) which are not admitted or denied i.e., that the claimant must prove, and (c) which allegations are admitted. If an allegation is denied, the defendant must (a) state his reason for denying it and (b) if he intends to put forward a different version of events, state his own version. In the case of a defendant who files a Defence, the court will serve a copy on the claimant and the case will be transferred to the defendant's local or "home" court, which will process the claim along the small claims track. If you expect the defendant to file a defence, you will save time if you issue your claim form in his local County Court.

Counterclaim: Part 20

The defendant may make a counterclaim as follows:

- This will be heard with the claim. A court fee will be payable
- If the counterclaim is above the small claims limit of £10,000 the district judge may allocate the claim to a different track.
- The defendant's counterclaim is a claim made by the defendant against the claimant, which may be less than his claim, so his claim is reduced, or it may be greater. A counterclaim is a separate action and an alternative to the defendant issuing his own claim form. Both claims are therefore managed in one action or set of proceedings. The defendant is in the same position as the claimant when making a counterclaim. The rules for the content of the counterclaim are the same as for any claim. The claimant must file a defence to the counterclaim to avoid judgement-in-default on the counterclaim. In this respect, the claimant

is for the purposes of the counterclaim in the same position as a defendant and the rules governing the content of the defence apply. Counterclaims are dealt with under Part 20. This Part also deals with claims by one defendant against another and circumstances in which a defendant wishes to issue proceedings against a non-party. If you as the defendant to a claim, or a defendant to a counterclaim, consider it to be applicable you should instruct a Solicitor.

Allocation to a Track: Allocation Questionnaire Form

If the defendant files a defence or counterclaim, the Court will:

- Post a form called an "Allocation Questionnaire" (N205A) TO THE PARTIES. This form records the details of the claim, the case number and date of service. The case number is now the reference point for your case and no steps can be taken without quoting it

- Both parties must complete and file the Allocation Questionnaire. The claimant must pay a fee when filing this form.

Directions Issued by the Court

After the Allocation Questionnaire is received, or in default of filing the Allocation Questionnaire, the court will allocate the claim to the small claims track and issue directions. These are the courts instructions as to how the case should proceed. District judges have wide powers to issue directions but for small claims PD27 provides standards form directions depending on the category of claim. The parties may apply for directions using form N244.

Enforcement Proceedings

If the defendant does not comply with a court order or judgement, you must take enforcement proceedings to enforce the judgement.

****

Chapter 7

The Legal System in Scotland and Northern Ireland

As explained, there are different legal systems in operation in Scotland and Northern Ireland. Both systems are 'Litigant in person friendly' and the respective websites dealing with the legal system offer help and assistance. The protocol for bringing or defending a case is very similar to the system in England and Wales. However, there are marked differences in bringing or defending a small claim, which are outlined below.

Scotland

The Court of Session is Scotland's highest civil court. It deals with all forms of civil cases, including delict (civil wrongs, referred to as "tort" in other jurisdictions), contract, commercial cases, judicial review, family law and intellectual property. Judges will hear all kinds of cases, but some will have specialisations, and there are arrangements for commercial cases. All appeals will go to the Supreme Court of the UK. The Court of Session is divided into the Outer House and the Inner House. The Outer House hears cases at first instance (meaning cases that have not previously been to court), and the Inner House is primarily the appeal court, hearing civil appeals from both the Outer House and Sheriff Courts. Appeals from the Inner House may go to the Supreme Court of the United Kingdom.

In the Outer House, a judge sits alone, but occasionally there may be a civil jury made up of 12 people. The Inner House cases are heard by three judges, although five or more judges may hear more complex and significant cases.

The High Court of Justiciary is Scotland's supreme criminal court. When sitting at first instance as a trial court, it hears the most serious criminal cases, such as murder and rape. A single judge hears cases with a jury of 15 people. At first instance, it sits in cities and larger towns around Scotland, but as an appeal court, it sits mostly in Edinburgh. The High Court hears criminal appeals from first instance cases from the High Court itself, Sheriff Courts, and Justice of the Peace Courts.

Most cases are dealt with in the country's Sheriff Courts unless they are of sufficient seriousness to go to the Supreme Courts at first instance. Criminal cases are heard by a sheriff and a jury (solemn procedure) but can be heard by a sheriff alone (summary procedure). Civil matters are also heard by a sheriff sitting alone.

The Sheriff Appeal Court was established on 22 September 2015 to hear appeals arising out of summary criminal proceedings from both the sheriff and justice of the peace courts. The Bench generally comprises two or three appeal sheriffs, depending on the type of appeal to be considered. The Court also hears appeals against bail decisions made by a sheriff or a justice of the peace. These hearings are presided over by a single appeal sheriff. The criminal court sits in the courthouse at Lawnmarket, Edinburgh, while the civil court sits in Parliament House, Edinburgh. Civil appeals are heard by a bench of three appeal sheriffs sitting in Edinburgh, although procedural business, routine appeals and appeals from small claims and summary causes may be dealt with by a single appeal sheriff in the local sheriffdom.

Less serious criminal matters are heard in Justice of the Peace Courts at first instance (equivalent of Magistrates Courts). The JP courts are in the same cities as the Sheriff Courts, but there are additional JP courts in other locations throughout Scotland. From 2008 to early 2010, Justice of the Peace Courts gradually replaced the former District Courts which were operated by local authorities.

Information on raising actions, and further details on each court's jurisdiction can be found on the Scottish Courts and Tribunals Service website www.scotcourts.gov.uk.

Other Courts in Scotland

The Court of the Lord Lyon - deals with matters of heraldry.

The Scottish Land Court - deals with disputes between landlord and tenant in relation to agricultural tenancies and crofting.

Hierarchy of Courts in Scotland

Civil Court

The Supreme Court of the United Kingdom
Court of Session
Sheriff Court

Criminal Courts

High Court of Justiciary
Sheriff Court
District Court
Justice of the Peace Courts

Tribunals and Special Courts

Tribunals
Children's Hearings
Court of the Lord Lyon
Court Martial
General assembly of the Church of Scotland

**

Small claims in Scotland-Simple Procedure

What is Simple Procedure?

Simple procedure is a court process designed to provide a speedy, inexpensive, and informal way to resolve disputes. A claim is made in the sheriff court by a claimant. The party against whom the claim is made is known as a respondent. The final decision in a claim is made by a sheriff or a summary sheriff. A person does not need to use a solicitor to use the simple procedure, but they can do if you wish. Where the value of the claim is over £5,000 the ordinary cause procedure should be followed. (see below)

What do I need to do before making a claim?

Before completing the claim form, it is important that you have tried to settle the dispute. This could mean writing to the person or company you have the dispute with and trying to agree a settlement.

Another option that may help you settle the dispute, before you decide to complete the claim form, is Alternative Dispute Resolution (ADR). Further information on ADR can be found on the mygov.scot website. ADR is also something that the sheriff or summary sheriff may refer you to after you have sent your claim form to the court as a way of settling the dispute out of court. Other things you might wish to consider before making a claim are:

- Is the person likely to be able to pay?

- If a company, has it ceased trading?
- Are you raising the claim against the correct person/company?
- Can you afford the time to prepare your case for the court hearing if the claim is defended?
- Can you afford to pay the cost of having any decision made in your favour enforced if it is not complied with as the court cannot do this for you?

How do I make a claim?

If you have exhausted all your options and wish to make a claim, you will need to complete a Claim Form (Form 3A). This should be completed and submitted electronically using the SCTS civil online portal.

If you feel that you cannot submit your claim electronically, you must seek the approval of the sheriff for the claim to proceed in paper format. To do so, you should send a note to the court, along with two copies of a completed claim form and relevant fee.

You will need to pay a fee to the court when submitting your claim form. The current fees can be accessed in the Sheriff Court Fees_ section. You may be entitled to fee exemption, for example, if you receive certain state benefits. Further information can be found in the court fees section of the website

*

How do I respond to a claim?

If a claim is made against you, the first formal notice you will receive is a copy of the completed claim form. Contained in the same envelope will be a response form (Form 4A). This usually comes by recorded delivery post but you may also receive it from a sheriff officer. The claim form contains the details of the claim made against you. If you wish to either:

- dispute the claim,
- admit liability for the claim and ask the court for time to pay; or
- admit liability for the claim and settle it before the last date for a response
- you should fill in Form 4A and send it to both the court and the claimant by the last date for a response.

Part 4 of the simple procedure explains how you respond to a claim and what the court will do with your response. Part 5 explains how you may ask for time to pay if the claim is for payment of a sum of money and how the claimant can consent or object to that.

Please note that staff in the Scottish Courts and Tribunals Service cannot give you legal advice, although they can help you to understand court procedures. You may wish to consult with and be represented in court by a solicitor, lay representative or courtroom supporter. Part 2 of the simple procedure explains about representatives and what they may and may not do.

What will happen to my case?

You may not need to attend court if:

- The respondent has not sent a response form

- The respondent has settled the claim before the last date for a response

- The claimant and the respondent have agreed payment terms about the payment of the claim

You may need to attend court if:

- The claimant has not accepted the offer of payment detailed in a response form

- The respondent wishes to defend all or part of the claim

- The sheriff or summary sheriff wishes to discuss certain matters about the claim

Should you need to attend court, you will be informed of the reasons, date and time of any hearing or discussion that the court has fixed.

You may be worried about attending court, particularly if you do not have a solicitor or other representative to speak for you. The following may help you to prepare:

- Part 7 of the simple procedure explains what happens after a response form is received or if no response form is received.

- Part 8 of the simple procedure explains the orders that a sheriff or summary sheriff can give to manage or decide a case.

- Part 21 contains a glossary explaining the meaning of certain legal words and expressions used in simple procedure.

Further Information

If you would like further information on simple procedure, please contact your local sheriff court. If you plan to visit the court to get further guidance or information it would be helpful to contact the court in advance to arrange a suitable time to do this, for example, outside busy court times. It would also be helpful to mention whether you have any special access or communication support needs. Contact your local sheriff court. Citizens Advice Bureau can also assist you. You can find contact details for your local office on the Citizens Advice Bureau website

Where can I get legal advice?

Scottish Courts and Tribunals Service staff cannot give you legal advice as they are not legally qualified. If you do need legal advice, the Law Society of Scotland can provide contact details for solicitors in your area. See the Law Society of Scotland website for further information- www.lawscot.org.uk

*

Ordinary Cause-What is the ordinary cause procedure?

The Ordinary Cause procedure can be used in the sheriff court where the value of the claim is over £5000. It is also the procedure used in the sheriff court for several other actions for example family actions, including divorce, dissolution of civil partnership, applications for orders relating to children e.g., residence and contact. The procedure is quite complex, and the Scottish Courts and Tribunals Service would therefore advise applicants to seek legal advice.

Which forms do I need to use?

There is no set application form to be completed when applying using the ordinary cause procedure; instead, it is raised using an initial writ. There are styles available within the Ordinary Cause Rules, and can be accessed at:

- Initial Writ Form G1 (including Personal Injury Actions in the all-Scotland sheriff court at Edinburgh)
- Initial Writ Form G1A (Commercial Actions)
- Initial Writ Form PI1 (Personal Injury Actions in the sheriff court (other than the all-Scotland sheriff court at Edinburgh))

How much does it cost?

Court fees are payable for lodging these applications in court, and the current fees can be accessed in the Sheriff Court Fees Section (Please note that separate fees are payable for personal injury cases in the all-Scotland sheriff court at Edinburgh). You may be entitled to fee exemption, for example if you are entitled to certain state benefits. Further information can be found in the Court Fees section and in the Fee Exemption Application Form.

You should note that these fees do not include any fees you may need to pay if you have instructed a solicitor to help you. The solicitor can give you information on these costs.

Where can I get legal advice?

Scottish Courts and Tribunals Service staff are not legally qualified and therefore cannot provide you with any legal advice. If you do need legal advice, the Law Society of Scotland_can provide contact details for solicitors in your area.

The justice system in Northern Ireland

Northern Ireland has its own judicial system which is headed by the Lord Chief Justice of Northern Ireland. The Department of Justice is responsible for the administration of the courts, which it runs through the Northern Ireland Courts and Tribunals Service. The Department also has responsibility for policy and legislation about criminal law, legal aid policy, the police, prisons, and probation.

Criminal and civil justice in Northern Ireland

Criminal law is about protecting the community and establishing and maintaining social order. The criminal law presumes that everyone is innocent until proven guilty. The level of proof that is required is that the evidence presented should show the person's guilt 'beyond reasonable doubt'. Civil law is mostly about disputes between individuals or corporate bodies. Cases must be proved on the balance of probabilities (more than a 50 per cent probability that the defendant is liable) rather than the 'beyond reasonable doubt' standard applied in criminal cases. In both criminal and civil cases, the courts make decisions on an adversarial rather than an inquisitorial basis. This means that both sides test the credibility and reliability of the evidence their opponent presents to the court. The judge or jury makes decisions based on the evidence presented.

Courts in Northern Ireland

UK Supreme Court	hears appeals on points of law in cases of major public importance
The Court of Appeal	hears appeals on points of law in criminal and civil cases from all courts
The High Court	hears complex or important civil cases and appeals from county court
County Courts	hears a wide range of civil actions including

	small claims and family cases
The Crown Court	hears all serious criminal cases
Magistrates Courts (including Youth Courts and Family Proceedings)	hears less serious criminal cases, cases involving juveniles and civil and family cases
The Enforcement of Judgments Office	enforces civil judgements

Agencies involved in the justice system

The justice system in Northern Ireland is made up of several agencies who are responsible for the administration of justice, maintaining law and order, detecting and stopping crime, dealing with offenders and overseeing the work of prisons. These are:

Police Service of Northern Ireland

Public Prosecution Service

Northern Ireland Courts and Tribunals Service

Northern Ireland Prison Service

Probation Board for Northern Ireland

Forensic Science Northern Ireland

Criminal Justice Inspection Northern Ireland

Youth Justice Agency

There are also several national crime bodies that work across the UK:

National Crime Agency

Serious Fraud Office (external link opens in a new window / tab)

UK Visas and Immigration

Border Force

Small claims process in Northern Ireland

The small claims process in Northern Ireland allows certain types of claims to be decided informally by the County Court, usually without the need of a solicitor or barrister.

Small claims

In general, a small claim is one where the value to be claimed is not more than £3,000 and which does not relate to personal injuries, road traffic accidents, libel or slander, title to land, legacy or annuity or any property of a marriage. If the total sum at issue between the same parties exceeds £3,000, the claimant must either:

- proceed by abandoning any amount due over £3,000 (this will be expressly noted)
- issue a civil bill in the County Court for a full hearing (up to £30,000)
- The Civil Processing Centre, in Laganside Courts, processes all cases initially, but if a case is disputed it is then

transferred to the office that is specified within the original application for hearing.

There are two types of small claim:

- liquidated - where the amount of claim is set, for example, loans or goods and services not paid for

- unliquidated - where the amount is estimated, for example, damage to property, faulty goods, or workmanship

Once a case has been submitted to the Civil Processing Centre and verified, the respondent (the person against whom the claim is made) is then posted a small claims pack giving all relevant information in relation to the case, including a copy of the completed small claims application form.

The court does not pay the amount that is awarded; it only decides who is liable. A Decree or Order made by the Small Claims Court is a County Court Judgment (CCJ) and may affect a respondent's credit status. It may also affect an applicant's credit status if a successful counterclaim is made.

Enforcement of Judgments Office

Before beginning the small claim process, the Enforcement of Judgments Office can search for a person or firm for a small fee. This will show if there are any enforced judgments already in existence against the respondent within the last six years. You can then use this information to help you to decide whether it would be practical for you to proceed with this action.

Even if you succeed with your claim, if the respondent has other judgments lodged with the Enforcement of Judgments Office, you may find that you will not get your money back immediately, if at all.

Fees

The fee for your small claim application will depend on the amount you wish to claim. If your claim is successful, the respondent will be ordered to pay you the amount decided by the Judge, plus the application fee along with any other costs awarded. If you are not successful, the respondent will not be ordered to pay you anything and you will not receive your fee back.

Small claims online

Much the same as England and Wales, this service allows the public and businesses to make a small claims application outside normal working hours and track the progress of the application online.

****

Useful addresses

Crown Prosecution Service

102 Petty France

London SW1H 9EA

www.cps.gov.uk

Email: enquiries@cps.gov.uk

HM Courts and Tribunal Service

102 Petty France

London SW1H 9EA

https://www.gov.uk/government/organisations/hm-courts-and-tribunals-service

Legal Action Group (LAG)

48 Chancery Lane

London

WC2A 1JF

Tel: 020 7833 2931

 Email: lag@lag.org.uk

The Legal Aid Agency

16 King Street

Nottingham NG1 2HS

0300 200 2020

https://www.gov.uk/government/organisations/legal-aid-agency

National Association of Citizen Advice Bureaus

www.citizensadvice.org

Legal Aid for Deaf People

www.royaldeaf.org.uk.

Free Representation Unit

5th Floor Kingsbourne House,

229-231 High Holborn,

London, WC1V 7DA |

Tel: 0207 611 9555

www. thefru.org.uk

The Chartered Institute of Legal Executives

Kempston Manor

Kempston

Bedford MK42 7AB

Tel: 01234 841000

www.cilex.org.uk

The Law Society

Tel: 020 7320 5650

www.lawsociety.org.uk

****

Glossary of terms

Acknowledgement of service-Form of reply to, or acknowledgement of, a service of court papers.

Acquittal-Discharge of defendant following verdict or direction of not guilty.

Adjourned generally-Temporary suspension of the hearing of a case by a court for a short period.

Advocate-A barrister or solicitor representing a person in court.

Affidavit-A written statement of evidence on oath or by affirmation to be true.

Appeal-Application to a higher court or authority for a review of a lower court decision.

Appellant-Person who appeals

Attachment of earnings-An order that directs an employer of a debtor to deduct a regular amount from salary or wages to pay off a debt.

Bail-Release of a defendant from custody until his or her appearance in court, usually based on financial security.

Bar-The collective term for barristers

Barrister-A member of the bar, that part of the legal profession that has rights of audience before a judge.

Bench warrant-A warrant issued by a judge for the arrest of an absent defendant.

Bill of indictment-A written statement of the charges against a defendant on trial in the Crown Court and signed by an officer of the court.

Brief-Written instructions to counsel to appear at a hearing of a party prepared by the solicitor and setting out the case and any case law relied upon.

Chambers-Either a private room or court where the public are not allowed and where the judge hears a case or offices used by a barrister.

Circuit judge-A judge who sits in the County and/or High Court.

Civil matters-Matters concerning private rights and not offences of the state.

Claim-Proceedings issued in the County or High Courts which initiate an action.

Claimant-The person issuing the claim, previously known as the plaintiff.

Committal-Committal for trial or sentence or an order to be committed to prison.

Common law-The law established over time by precedent.

Conditional discharge-A discharge of a convicted defendant without sentence on condition that he or she does not re-offend within a period.

Co-respondent-A person named as an adulterer (or third person) in a divorce.

Counsel-A Barrister

Counterclaim-A claim made by a defendant against a claimant in a case.

County Court-County courts deal with civil matters including all small claims up to £15,000.

Court of Appeal-Divided into civil and criminal divisions and hears appeals from the High court and the County court.

Crown Court-The Crown Court deals with all crimes committed for judgement to the magistrate's court and also hears appeals in cases heard by the magistrate's court.

Damages-An amount of money claimed as compensation for physical or material loss e.g., personal injury

Defendant-The person standing trial, the person being sued.

Deposition-A statement of evidence written down and sworn or affirmed.

Determination-The scrutiny of a bill of costs in criminal proceedings to determine that the amounts claimed are reasonable.

Discovery of documents-The mutual disclosure of evidence and information held by each side relating to a case.

District judge-A judicial officer of the court.

Exhibit-Item or document referred to in an affidavit or used during the court trial or hearing.

Expert witness-Person employed to give evidence on a subject or matter on which they are knowledgeable and qualified.

Fiat-A decree or command

Garnishee-A summons issued by a claimant against a third party for seizure of money or assets in their keeping.

High Court-A civil court which consists of three divisions, the Queens Bench Division, hearing civil disputes, Family Division concerning matrimonial and child related matters and the Chancery dealing with property and fraud related matters.

Indictable offence-A criminal offence triable only by the Crown Court.

Injunction-An order of the court either restraining a person from carrying out a course of action or directing a course of action to be complied with.

Judge-An officer appointed to administer the law and who has the authority to hear and try cases in a court of law.

Jury-A body of jurors sworn to reach a verdict according to evidence presented in court.

Justice of the peace-A lay-magistrate or person appointed to administer business in a magistrate's court. Also sits in the crown court with a judge or a recorder to hear appeals and commute sentences.

Law lords-Describes the judges of the House of Lords.

Legal aid/help-Facility to obtain aid towards fees and expenses relating to court cases.

Libel-A written and published statement/article which contains damaging remarks about another person's character and reputation.

Litigation-Legal proceedings.

Lord Chancellor-The cabinet minister who acts as speaker of the House of Lords and oversees the hearings of the Law Lords. Has other wide responsibilities.

Lord Chief Justice-Senior judge of the Court of Appeal Criminal Division and heads the Queens Bench Division of the High Courts of Justice.

Magistrates Court-A court where criminal proceedings are commenced. Also has jurisdiction to deal with a range of civil matters.

Master of the Rolls-Senior judge of the Court of Appeal Criminal Division.

Mitigation-Reasons submitted on behalf of a guilty party to excuse or partly excuse the offence committed to minimise the sentence.

Motion-An application by one party to the High Court for a judgement in their favour.

Notary public-Someone who is authorised to swear oaths and execute deeds.

Oath-A verbal promise by a person of religious beliefs to tell the truth.

Official solicitor-A solicitor or barrister appointed by the Lord Chancellor working in the Lord Chancellors office. The duties include

133

looking after the affairs of people who cannot look after affairs due to incapacity i.e. mental illness.

Oral examination-A method of questioning a person under oath before an officer of the court to obtain details of their financial affairs.

Order-A direction of the court.

Particulars Of Claim-Details relevant to a case

Party-Any of the participants in a court case.

Penal notice-Directions attached to a court order if breach of that order result in imprisonment.

Personal application-Application made to the court without legal representation.

Plea-A defendants reply to a charge.

Pleadings-Documents setting out the claim or defence of parties involved in legal proceedings.

Precedent-The decision of a case which has established principles, and which can be used as authority for a future case.

Pre-trial review-A preliminary appointment at which the district judge examines the issues and issues directions and a timetable for the case.

Queens Counsel-Barristers of at least ten years standing, they take on work of importance and are know as 'Silks'.

Recorder-Members of the legal profession (barristers or solicitors) who are appointed to act in a senior capacity on a part time basis and who may progress to the post of full-time judge.

Registrar-Known now as district judge and deputy district judges they are active in the county courts.

Right of audience-Entitlement to appear in front of a court in a legal capacity and conduct proceedings.

Solicitor-Member of the legal profession chiefly concerned with representing clients and preparing cases.

Summary judgement-Judgement obtained from the claimant where there is no defence or no valid grounds for defence.

Summing up-A review of the evidence by representatives of the claimant and defendant before the jury retires to give its verdict.

Tort-A civil wrong committed against a person for which compensation may be sought.

Verdict-The finding of guilty or not guilty by a jury.

Witness-A person who gives evidence to court.

****

Index

Barrister, 18, 40, 128, 129
British legal system, 17

Circuit judges, 82
Civil cases, 3, 6, 18, 19, 28, 84
Civil Procedure Rules, 5, 82
Claim Production Centre, 101
Claimant, 18, 129
Companies House, 98
Coronavirus, 10, 11
Counterclaim, 102, 105
County Court Money Claims Centre, 97, 101
County Courts Act 1846, 81
Court Reporter, 70
COVID 19, 7, 10, 140
Criminal Bar Association (CBA, 14
Criminal cases, 3, 20
Criminal Injuries Compensation Authority, 55
Crown Courts, 19, 34, 63, 92
Crown Prosecution Service, 5, 20, 66, 67, 84, 125

Damages, 4, 19, 54, 55, 130
Defence, 102, 104, 105
Defendant, 18, 68, 130

Employment Appeals Tribunal, 34

Freezing Orders, 101

High Court, 101

House of Lords, 27, 132

indictment, 20, 128

Judgement in Default, 104
Jury, 61, 62, 64, 132

Lands Tribunal, 34
Legal aid, 132
Litigant in person, 19
Lord Chancellor's homepage, 96

Magistrates, 19, 27, 133
Matrimonial Causes Act 1967, 83
Money Claims On-Line, 97
Nightingale Courts, 11

Pandemic, 10, 12, 13, 15, 62, 140, 141, 142, 143, 144, 146

Registrars, 5, 82
Remote courts, 10

Small claims in the county court, 3, 6, 32
Small Claims procedure, 84
Solicitor, 18, 41, 135

The Chancery Division, 3, 34
The county court, 3
The Court of Appeal, 3, 34
The Crown Court, 130
The Family Division, 3, 34
The High Court, 3, 33
The Law Society, 40, 126

The Queens Bench Division, 3, 34
The small claims track, 33
Tribunals, 6, 84

Using a solicitor, 42

Victims of crime, 55

Witnesses, 5, 68, 79
Writ, 18

Appendix One

A Summary of the ongoing Review of the Justice System in the United Kingdom in 2022. This is particularly relevant following the pandemic and the impact of COVID 19.

A justice system for those who need it most

Our justice system defends our fundamental rights and freedoms. It is a cornerstone of our modern society, and it must serve all those who call on it, when they call on it. From some of the most vulnerable people in our society, to families in crisis, victims of crime, claimants, and commercial businesses – we have a responsibility to administer a justice system that is accessible to everyone and operates efficiently.

This reform means more and better ways to access justice for all those who need it, quicker and simpler processes for professional and public court users alike and a workforce that is as effective as it can possibly be. It means giving judges more time to do their job by cutting down on unnecessary paperwork and reserving court time for the most complex cases. It means making justice easier.

Modernising now to build a solid foundation for the future

As well as protecting and upholding the rights of citizens, our justice system is the envy of the world, attracting billions of pounds of business each year as people all over the globe choose to have their cases heard in a fair and independent system, proven over centuries. But significant parts remain antiquated – with paper-based, complicated systems that were not designed around the people who use them. It is out of step with the modern world.

We have been modernising our services since 2016, providing new, user-friendly digital services and improving efficiency at the same time. The original vision for reform - to modernise and upgrade our justice system so that it works even better for everyone - remains true. But we must recognise that the world has changed since 2016 – and rapidly so – because of the COVID-19 pandemic that started in 2020.

To simply be able to keep our courts operating, we have had to adapt quickly and make immediate changes to our ways of working and our technology. It is now even clearer that we need to finish our programme of reform so we can recover from the impacts of the pandemic, ensure our future resilience and provide a platform for future development to meet the demands of an ever-changing society.

Progress so far

Reform is already well under way and having a huge impact for the public. Over 426,000 people have used our online services, keeping simple claims out of court and reserving judges and court space for the most difficult cases. We now have online services for appealing immigration and asylum decisions, disputing benefits decisions and for local authorities to apply to take children into care. All of this

142

helps some of the most vulnerable people facing difficult situations get justice as quickly as possible and supports litigants who do not have legal representation.

Our single justice procedure deals with simple, non-imprisonable cases (such as speeding of fare-evasion) out of court. It minimises delay and frees up court time for those cases that need to be heard in court. For anyone pleading guilty to an offence, it means they don't have to attend court and their case is likely to be dealt with faster and more efficiently.

We're starting to roll out our brand-new digital platform to manage 1.5m annual criminal cases. It means victims will see justice more quickly and we will be able to manage the surge in demand brought about by 20,000 new police officers.

Reform in a time of COVID-19

We have come a long way, but the case for continued modernisation is more compelling than ever. The pandemic has shone a light on courts and tribunals and highlighted that the most resilient services are those where there has been investment, where we have introduced digital options for users, and new technology to facilitate alternative ways of working. The antiquated systems that necessitated the need for reform in the first place have been exposed as fragile in the face of an extremely challenging environment.

Online services, remote hearing capability and paperless systems have all played their part in reducing the need for people to visit sites in person and be able to follow their cases, do their jobs or file information online.

Without the modernisation that has already happened, large parts of the system such as probate and divorce would have almost ground to a halt. Instead, divorce performance is the best it has been in years. The Special Educational Needs and Disability tribunal has been running as a completely remote hearing since the start of the pandemic. This means families in crisis, often with children with complex needs, can seek justice quickly and easily.

Put simply, reform is important to our recovery. It has enabled us to keep the wheels of justice turning during the pandemic. And it will help us tackle the longer-term impact of the pandemic.

Foundations fit for the future

Modernisation is not just the means to respond to, and recover from, the unique challenges of the pandemic. It is the foundation for a new world of improved access to justice, where rising demand is met, and disputes are resolved quickly without the need to go to court.

Our ambition – regardless of the pandemic – has always been to play our part in establishing a modern justice system. And there is still more work to do. We are working on improvements so people can make money claims for an unspecified amount, apply for adoption, enter child custody cases and resolve possession claims, all online. Paper forms will be shorter, in plain language, and paid staff will be on hand to help online and by phone. We will complete the national roll-out of the Common Platform, providing a single case management system for criminal courts and CPS. This means the most serious cases will be supported by the modern infrastructure it deserves. We will have efficient, digital courts, with new IT systems and screens, as befits any modern service. Our new scheduling and listing tools will enable us to list cases more efficiently and to provide detailed data on how we use our valuable court space.

Our reform – and our response to, and recovery from, the effects of the pandemic – will be the foundation on which we build a justice system that is fit for this bold new future. A system that plays its part in the stability of society and the smooth running of the economy. And one in which the public, court users, the judiciary and legal professionals, all have absolute confidence.

Jurisdictional fact sheets and case summaries

Our fact sheets provide and case summaries more information on what's happening in different jurisdictions.

Engaging with others

We engage with a range of other stakeholders, including professional and public user groups, who work with us on aspects of the reform programme as well as collaborating on new development proposals.

****

Appendix 2

Courts and tribunals: living with COVID-19

Applies to England, Scotland, and Wales

Following the government publishing new guidance on living with respiratory infections including COVID-19, we have been able to remove many of the safety measures put in place during the pandemic in England. We continue to follow government and public health guidance and the different rules in Wales and Scotland.

Coming to a court or tribunal

Our courts and tribunals in England, Scotland and Wales meet required safety standards and are open for hearings. You should attend your hearing as planned.

If you have symptoms of a respiratory infection, such as COVID-19, have a high temperature or do not feel well enough to attend a hearing, you are advised to contact the court or tribunal immediately. You should ask the court or tribunal to consider alternative arrangements. In most cases people who are ill, who have COVID-19 symptoms, or who have tested positive, should not come to our buildings, as this helps to protect others. The court or tribunal will consider individual requests on a case-by-case basis.

Custody suites

Our additional safety measures will remain in place in line with HM Prisons and Probation Service guidance. Fluid resistant safety masks are Personal Protective Equipment rather than face coverings and are still required in custody suites and by Court and Tribunal Security Officers undertaking certain roles. These measures should not restrict capacity. Defendants will be encouraged to wear face coverings, but this is not mandatory.

Jury service

We will continue to provide local lateral flow testing kits for jurors. Jurors will no longer be required to wear fluid resistant surgical masks in smaller rooms and will be able to eat and drink in those rooms.

Face coverings

Face coverings are no longer mandatory in any parts of our buildings in England and Wales, though the position in custody suites is set out above. Court and tribunal users can continue to wear face coverings in any of our buildings should they choose to do so.

In Scotland, it remains mandatory for court and tribunal users to wear face coverings while in our buildings.

Local assessments

Staff in our buildings work hard to ensure your safety. You can raise any issues in our buildings with local managers.

Keep up to date

We update you on the operational running of our courts and tribunals through:

- advice on GOV.UK
- our weekly operational update
- our find a court or tribunal service
- our HMCTS Twitter channel

****

www.straightforwardco.co.uk

All titles, listed below, in the Straightforward Guides Series can be purchased online, using credit card or other forms of payment by going to www.straightfowardco.co.uk A discount of 25% per title is offered with online purchases.

Law

A Straightforward Guide to:

Consumer Rights

Bankruptcy Insolvency and the Law

Employment Law

Private Tenants Rights

Civil Justice After COVID

Family law

Small Claims in the County Court

Contract law

Intellectual Property and the law

Divorce and the law

Leaseholders Rights

The Process of Conveyancing

Knowing Your Rights and Using the Courts

Producing Your own Will

Housing Rights

Bailiffs and the law

Probate and The Law

Company law

What to Expect When You Go to Court

Give me Your Money-Guide to Effective Debt Collection

Caring for a Disabled Child

General titles

Letting Property for Profit

Buying, Selling and Renting property

Buying a Home in England and France

Bookkeeping and Accounts for Small Business

Creative Writing

Freelance Writing

Writing Your own Life Story

Writing performance Poetry

Writing Romantic Fiction

Speech Writing

Creating a Successful Commercial Website

The Straightforward Business Plan
The Straightforward C.V.

Successful Public Speaking

Handling Bereavement

Individual and Personal Finance

Understanding Mental Illness

Crime Reference

The Crime Writers casebook

Being a Detective

Catching a Killer

A Comprehensive Guide to Arrest and Detention

A Comprehensive Guide to Burglary and Robbery

A Comprehensive Guide to Drink and Disorder

Go to:

www.straightforwardco.co.uk

****

How to be a Litigant in Person in The New legal World

Representing Yourself in The Civil Courts

Michael Langford

ISBN: 978-1-84716-716-3

This is the ideal companion volume to this book, available at all good bookshops.

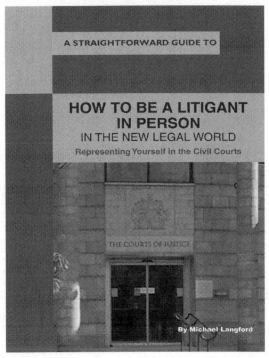